The Professional Cloud Architect's Big Fact Sheet

Yaron Hollander

econom☁.tech

The Professional Cloud Architect's Big Fact Sheet
by Yaron Hollander

Copyright 2020 Yaron Hollander

This publication is protected under copyright. All rights reserved. No part of this publication may be reproduced, transmitted, copied, photocopied, recorded, stored, retrieved or shared, without permission in writing from the author.

Clarification and disclaimer

The technologies, methodologies, services and products reviewed in this book are the intellectual property of Google and their official partners. The author describes them solely from the perspective of a user. The author does not have access to any information from Google which is not already in the public domain. The author does not hold any rights or interests related to the Google Cloud Platform, other than the interest of sharing good practices in the professional community.

The author has made genuine efforts to include helpful advice in this book, but this is not a formal source of guidance regarding the Google Cloud Platform. The book describes the views of the author and reflects his professional judgement. The author cannot guarantee that the coverage of the relevant topics in this book is accurate or complete.

Readers must always use their judgement and consult with other sources, including formal documentation published by Google and its official partners, when deciding whether, when and how to use the advice provided here.

Anyone using information from this book should consider the safety, security, legality and professionalism of their actions. They must seek professional advice that is specific to the situation where the information is being used, because the advice provided in the book is general. The author cannot be held responsible or accept liability for any damage or harm that may result from the way you use this book.

Contents

1	**Introduction**		**1**
	1.1	What is this book	1
	1.2	Abbreviations	2
	1.3	Things you should know already	3
	1.4	The cloud language	6
2	**GCP basics**		**14**
	2.1	Where is this cloud	14
	2.2	Your GCP resources	19
	2.3	Accessing your resources	26
	2.4	GCP brands	30
3	**Compute services**		**33**
	3.1	Google Compute Engine	33
	3.2	Managing your VMs	35
	3.3	Paying for your VMs	37
	3.4	More about your VMs	39
	3.5	Right-sizing	40
	3.6	Migrating on-prem VMs to GCE	41
	3.7	Google Cloud Functions	42
	3.8	Google App Engine	43
	3.9	Cloud Endpoints	45
	3.10	Apigee	46
	3.11	Cloud Pub/Sub	47
	3.12	Cloud Tasks	49
	3.13	Cloud TPU	50
4	**Container services**		**51**
	4.1	What's a container	51
	4.2	Google Kubernetes Engine	52
	4.3	GKE storage types and workload types	54
	4.4	GKE networking	56
	4.5	Interacting with GKE	59
	4.6	GKE operations	59
	4.7	Extensions to GKE	61

	4.8	Serverless containers	64
	4.9	Service mesh	65

5 Storage services — 69
	5.1	Traditional storage on GCP	69
	5.2	Google Cloud Storage	73
	5.3	Securing your GCS objects	77
	5.4	Interacting with GCS	79
	5.5	Transfer services	83
	5.6	Payment mindsets	85

6 Databases — 93
	6.1	The database language	93
	6.2	Cloud SQL	99
	6.3	Cloud Spanner	100
	6.4	Cloud Bigtable	102
	6.5	Firebase Realtime Database	105
	6.6	Cloud Firestore	106
	6.7	BigQuery	108
	6.8	Cloud Memorystore	113
	6.9	Choosing your database	114

7 Data services — 117
	7.1	Interactive data services	117
	7.2	Hiring a cluster	120
	7.3	Data pipeline services	123
	7.4	Artificial intelligence	128
	7.5	Services for specific sectors	141

8 Networking services — 144
	8.1	Virtual Private Cloud	144
	8.2	VPC routing	147
	8.3	Firewalls	149
	8.4	Network sharing and peering	150
	8.5	Principles of load balancing	152
	8.6	Types of load balancing	156
	8.7	Cloud DNS	163
	8.8	IP addresses	165

	8.9	Cloud NAT	167
	8.10	Cloud Router	168
	8.11	Cloud VPN	170
	8.12	Cloud Interconnect	172
	8.13	Cloud CDN	176
9	**Security services**		**178**
	9.1	Cloud IAM	178
	9.2	Other identity and access services	182
	9.3	Data Loss Prevention	187
	9.4	Managing keys and secrets	188
	9.5	Protection from threats	192
	9.6	Regulatory compliance	199
10	**System operation**		**203**
	10.1	Continuous delivery	203
	10.2	Logging and monitoring	208
	10.3	Resource catalogs	214
11	**Exam preparation**		**216**
	11.1	Exam case studies	216
	11.2	Exam tips	218

Chapter 1
Introduction

1.1 What is this book

This book is based on the notes I took when preparing for the "Google Cloud Certified - Professional Cloud Architect" exam. Yes, I passed it, thanks for asking. I kept updating these notes based on things I learned as an architect designing Google Cloud solutions. I'm offering you my notes in case you are preparing for this exam, or for a job interview in a similar area of work, or as a general reference if you use the **Google Cloud Platform** (**GCP**).

When I took these notes, I wasn't trying to explain everything in detail. The wide topic of "GCP architecture" covers tons of facts and details, so I preferred to skip everything that I thought was either self-explanatory or just basic knowledge of technology. I focused on things which I found difficult and not obvious. I wanted to create a list of concise bullet points about the tricky aspects of GCP, without long stories.

It ended up quite long anyway, but this is the reality: to be a certified professional GCP architect you need to know a lot. This book still is extremely succinct, compared to the many hundreds of pages you'd need to read in Google's formal documentation. There is very little repetition in the book, and every word matters (except the bad jokes I added in a few places).

So if you are trying to learn about the range of GCP services from an architect's perspective, and you want a list of facts that go straight to the point, this book might help. You won't find here step-by-step examples or hands-on guidance. This book is about the stuff they ask about in the cloud architect exam and related job interviews: features, principles, architectural decisions.

You'll find two kinds of info in this book. In each chapter I go through individual GCP services and list things that are worth knowing about them; but occasionally I also look across services and compare them to each other. In an exam, interview or in the real world, you constantly face dilemmas choosing between competing options, so I tried to reflect this in this book. In the last chapter I've also included some exam tips.

I've tried to keep the info in this book up-to-date right until the day the book is published. But GCP changes often, so things will evolve by the time you read this. Also, I assembled so much material into this book, that I might have made a few mistakes. If you find any then, first, I apologise! And second, please email me (hello@economo.tech) to tell me about mistakes you've found so that I can correct them. If your correction is significant then I'll make sure to thank you in future versions. Please also check out my website, economo.tech, for updates.

1.2 Abbreviations

I find things easier to read if there aren't too many long words. So I chose several long words that repeat many times in this book, and I've replaced them with shorter ones:

- **Info** anywhere in this book means "information"
- **App** anywhere in this book means "application"
- **Org** anywhere in this book means "organisation"
- **Env** anywhere in this book means "environment"
- **Ops** anywhere in this book means "operations"
- **Config** anywhere in this book means "configuration"
- **On-prem** anywhere in this book means "on-premises"
- **Auto** anywhere in this book means "automatic"
- **Admin** anywhere in this book means "administrator"
- **IPs** anywhere in this book means "IP addresses"
- **(p52)** anywhere in this book means "see on page 52"

These abbreviations are used in this book, but don't use them anywhere else! An "org policy" is really an "organisation policy".

I use the following acronyms:

- **GCP** for Google Cloud Platform
- **GCE** for Google Compute Engine
- **GAE** for Google App Engine
- **GCF** for Google Cloud Functions
- **GKE** for Google Kubernetes Engine
- **GCS** for Google Cloud Storage

Also, each chapter has a colour, and I've used the colours when referring to other chapters.

1.3 Things you should know already

The following is a list of basic things you need to know already in order to start preparing yourself for work as a GCP architect. Just in case you're having a bad day, I'll give you a quick reminder before we move on to new things. My definitions are very simplified, on purpose. You can skip this section if you're confident enough.

- **Software**. Apps, websites, systems and products which are developed by writing code in a programming language.
- **Hardware**. Computers, electronic devices and other machines that software can run on. Hardware takes physical space.
- **Operating system**. The software that knows how to make direct use of your hardware, and acts as a translator when other pieces of software need anything from that hardware.
- **Network**. A mix of hardware and software that allows computers and other devices to send digital info to each other.
- **Data**. Info that is stored in a digital format on hardware, and is usually used by software.
- **Traffic**. Data that gets transferred across a network.
- **Compute**. The ability of hardware and software to process info in the way users require. Compute processes may involve reading and writing data, making calculations, evaluating whether certain conditions are met, and other things.
- **Storage**. The ability of hardware and software to keep data for an amount of time in the way users require.
- **Memory**. A relatively small amount of data storage space, which compute processes can access at a very high speed compared to other types of storage.
- **CPU**. The piece of hardware in a computer that gives it the ability to process info in the way required by software.
- **GPU**. An alternative to a CPU, that can run many processes in parallel and is powerful for graphics and some types of math.

- **Server**. This can be software which can be contacted over a network and has some compute or storage responsibilities. Or it can be the hardware that this server software sits on.
- **Client**. Any device, user or tool that is connected to a network and sometimes exchanges info with a server (like when a browser loads a website).
- **Service**. Anything that a server can give to a client when asked, such as: the ability to watch a movie; confirmation that a network is working; permission to access another server.
- **Micro-service**. Same thing as a service. This term is used when an advanced product is made of many services which are developed and operated in isolation, but can work together by knowing when and how to call each other.
- **Cloud**. A collection of services that let the user develop software while using the cloud provider's hardware.
- **Solution**. Software you build to meet specific requirements, possibly using some existing services, software and hardware.
- **Data centre**. The physical location of your servers. It may be run by your org, or by a cloud provider, or by someone else.
- **On-prem**. The physical location of your servers, if they are run by your own org, and not by a cloud provider.
- **KB**, **MB**, **GB**, **TB**, **PB**. Different units of data volume.
- **Mbps**, **Gbps**. Common units of data transfer speed, either Mb or Gb per second. There are 8 Mb in 1 MB, and 8 Gb in 1 GB.
- **Ingestion** or **ingress**. Bringing data into a system.
- **Egress**. Taking data out of a system.
- **IOPS**. Input and output ops per second. It's a measure of storage speed which doesn't consider file size.
- **Throughput**. Data volume transferred per second. It's a measure of storage speed which considers file size.
- **Metadata**. Data that describes data. For example, the size of a data file and the date when it was last changed.
- **Migration**. Taking a solution that works in one place (for example in your on-prem data centre) and making it work in a different place (for example in the cloud).

- **Development lifecycle**. Your solutions typically go through a lifecycle that may include a development phase, testing phase, and a "production" phase where the solution is in active use.
- **Command line**. An interactive interface with a minimalist appearance. Also called **CLI**. You type some code which it then tries to run using the relevant software.
- **UI**. A user interface, sometimes accessed via a web browser.
- **API**. A method of communication between different software systems. A system can "expose" some features or functions through its API, which other systems may then be able to use.
- **REST**. A common set of conventions for building APIs.
- **URL**. A human-readable address like "https://cnn.com/", that shows where and how to find a resource in a network.
- **Endpoint**. Info you add to a URL which defines the path that an API needs to take to find a specific resource.
- **Availability**. The ability of a service to keep running properly most of the time; or the proportion of time it runs properly.
- **Integrity**. The ability to ensure that systems and data have not been modified by anyone not authorised to do so.
- **Confidentiality**. The ability to ensure that info is only shared with those it was meant to be shared with.
- **Security**. The ability to maintain the confidentiality, integrity and availability of your solutions and data, even when there are people, orgs and external factors that make it difficult.
- **Authentication**. Establishing the identity of a user.
- **Authorisation**. Establishing the permissions of the user.
- **Latency**. The time it takes for info to be sent over a network.
- **Performance**. The ability to do a lot of work fast.
- **Cache**. A small amount of low-latency memory, where you store data that you're likely to re-use.
- **Failover**. Switching to another system when a system fails.
- **Durability**. The chance that data isn't lost over time.
- **Architecture**. A plan that describes how software, hardware, data, services and other components together make up a solution that meets the relevant requirements.
- **AWS**. The Amazon Web Services, a different cloud platform.

1.4 The cloud language

All the terms I listed in the previous section are basic ones, that you are meant to know already. The terms I explain in this section are slightly different. They are also basic, but it's OK if you are still less confident about these.

I call these terms "basic" not because they're simple (they're not), but because they are very common when talking about cloud-based solutions. They all have an important role when designing solutions using cloud services.

- **Virtual machine** (**VM**). A service you use as if it's a hardware device, but in fact it's software that runs on a **host** machine.
    - ▶ You can provision VMs in your own data centre or get them from a cloud provider; the latter is the most common form of "Infrastructure as a Service" (**IaaS**).
    - ▶ Running your services on VMs, instead of hosting them directly on physical servers, can replace much of your hardware config effort with software config effort.
    - ▶ This is often a good thing because it creates opportunities for more consistent version control, backup procedures and automation.
    - ▶ Real machines have a CPU (p3); VMs have a **vCPU**.
- **Managed service**. A service you get from a cloud provider is "managed" if it gives you more than just VMs.
    - ▶ The cloud provider may include in the service features such as automated backup, replication, scaling, monitoring, logging, periodic updates of the operating system, and security threat detection.
    - ▶ A service that lets you develop your solutions, while freeing you up from these related logistics, can be called "Platform as a Service" (**PaaS**).
- **Scaling**. A service you get from a cloud provider usually gives you the flexibility to change how much of it you consume in

terms of storage space, memory, compute power and other parameters.
- ▶ This is a major difference from running your own on-prem infrastructure.
- ▶ Common reasons why you might want to scale are changes to the amount of user activity; your desire to control costs; or a decision you make to merge or split your different services in a new way.
- ▶ You can scale up or down, to either increase or reduce the cloud resources you consume.
- ▶ Services such as VMs can scale **horizontally** (by performing the same task with more VMs or fewer VMs) and **vertically** (by performing the same task with a more powerful or less powerful machine).
- ▶ Some cloud services are scaled manually by changing config settings. Others are **auto-scaling**. With some services you can choose, auto or manual. See table 2.

■ **Replication**. The resources you host in a cloud can have copies in multiple data centres.
- ▶ This is much harder to achieve without using the cloud, because you'd need multiple data centres.
- ▶ Replication helps achieve **high availability** and **fault tolerance** in case one data centre fails for some reason.
- ▶ Replication may also reduce latency (p5), because your users can connect to the copy nearest to them.
- ▶ The term **redundancy** has a similar meaning.
- ▶ Replication gives **strong consistency** if it ensures there's never a conflict between the copies. This takes time to achieve so might come at the expense of availability (p5).
- ▶ Replication gives **eventual consistency** if the data is available even when some copies are still being updated.

■ **Serverless**. A cloud service is "serverless" if the cloud provider takes even more responsibility for the logistics than in a managed service (p6).
- ▶ Serverless resources are not server-less…! There is always a server involved, but your role in managing it is minimal.
- ▶ Feature like auto-scaling are provided with hardly any config work from your side.

▶ An important feature of serverless resources is that you pay directly per use. During periods when your service doesn't receive any requests, you pay nothing.

- **Software as a Service.** SaaS is the sister of IaaS (p6), PaaS (p6) and serverless (p7). But IaaS and PaaS are services you typically get from a cloud provider, whereas SaaS is a service that a much wider range of providers (maybe like your own company) offer to their customers.

  ▶ You use IaaS, PaaS or serverless to create solutions. SaaS might be the type of solution you create.

  ▶ Your solution is SaaS if it is web-based, accessed by users via their browser, licensed on a subscription basis, and often has some on-demand features.

- **Backend.** Users may see a service (p4) as one thing, but there's usually a split between the compute (p3) work users need, which is the backend, and the service itself, which helps users access the backend.

- **IP address.** A code you can attach to a resource, service or device on a network, which anyone connected to the same network can use when they want to get in touch.

  ▶ Version 4 of this approach (**IPv4**) is used globally. The code it attaches to resources is made of 4 numbers and can look like "169.254.169.25".

  ▶ When the network you use is the internet, the IP address is called "public" or "external". In a more local network you can use a "private" or "internal" IP address.

  ▶ The number of public IPv4 addresses is limited, so newer versions like **IPv6** are becoming common for global use.

  ▶ A local network usually has enough private IPv4 addresses (just like different cities can have a "14 Church Street").

  ▶ Resources in a cloud can have public addresses, private addresses, multiple addresses, or no address at all.

- **Port number.** To let multiple resources share one address, you use different ports. For example, if a VM hosts a server for HTTPS traffic, it will use port number 443. The same VM with the same IP address can serve other traffic on other ports.

- **Cluster**. A group of devices (such as VMs) that works in a coordinated way. It's quite common for all devices in a cluster to be of the same type of machine and located in one place.
- **Distributed system**. Any system where compute work is done in parallel across different devices, and sometimes also in different locations.
- **Hybrid**. This word has many meanings, but in GCP it is usually about a solution that combines resources both on-prem and in the cloud.
- **TCP** and **UDP**. Two common methods for transporting info across a network.
- **HTTP**. A common method of communication between apps. HTTP relies on a TCP connection.
- **SSH**. A common method for connecting into a remote machine in a secure way.
- **SSL** and **TLS**. Methods for adding security to communication over a network. Only TLS is used in practice, but people often call it SSL, so in this book I say "SSL" when I mean "TLS".
- **HTTPS**. A common method of communication between apps, using HTTP secured with SSL.
- **Certificate**. A file containing a code for authentication (p5) or other forms of verification, in methods such as SSL.
- **Certificate authority**. Someone that gives SSL certificates which others trust.
- **OAuth2**. A method for using the identity provided by one service when getting authorisation (p5) to access another service. For example, when you use your Facebook account to sign into a music streaming service.
- **JWT** (**JSON web token**). A file containing a code for authorisation (p5) in methods like OAuth2.
- **OpenID Connect**. An extension to OAuth2, used for sharing user info between the authentication service and the service the user gets access to.
- **Batch**. A batch process isn't interactive and doesn't run in real time while you wait. Often it needs more resources than

available in the computer's memory. It may be scheduled to run periodically, or as part of a queue of compute jobs to run.

- **Streaming data**. Data that may arrive continuously, so it can't be handled as a complete dataset and often needs to be processed in real time or in small frequent batches.

- **Event**. A party or gig in town in the weekend. Just kidding. Any change in a system can be an event, if you design the system to generate an event notification, which gets sent somewhere and may trigger an action. Event examples: button clicked; movie uploaded; new account created; holiday approved. Each type of event is twinned with an **event handler** that knows what action should be triggered.

- **Synchronous**. Anything that must be completed before you can move to the next thing. For example, if you sell something online, payment approval must be completed before you can confirm the purchase.

- **Asynchronous** (**async**). Anything that doesn't depend on getting an immediate response.
    - ▶ An async process can move on to the next step while the previous one is still running in parallel.
    - ▶ Async tasks are less sensitive than synchronous ones to the current state of other tasks.
    - ▶ This is why async tasks are easier to put in a queue and start running when compute resources become available.
    - ▶ The ability of cloud solutions to scale (p6) means that they work best when you design them to use async processing.

- **Logging**. The process where a service automatically creates a list ("log") of the ops (p2) it performed. You can inspect the log to learn whether the service works in the way you wanted.

- **Monitoring**. The practice of defining some metrics of how your service performs and checking these metrics regularly.

- **Ephemeral**. A short-lived resource, which only exists temporarily, like the data stored in the memory of a VM.

- **Persistence**. Retaining information so that it is not ephemeral and remains available for later re-use.
- **Load balancing**. Distributing compute work across multiple backends (p8) so that the overall system works efficiently.
- **CI/CD**. Continuous integration and continuous delivery. It's a group of working practices for teams developing solutions, involving significant automation and focus on the readiness to release the latest solution at any time.

Since we spoke about IaaS (p6), PaaS (p6) and serverless (p7), **table 1** lists some important GCP services and splits them into these types of services. And since we spoke about scaling (p6), **table 2** focuses on different types of scaling across those GCP services where scaling is relevant.

Don't be alarmed if you don't understand yet what each GCP service listed in these tables does; we'll cover this later. The colours of the text indicate which chapter in this book covers each of these GCP services.

Not all GCP services are included in tables 1 and 2, since some do not fit comfortably into any of the categories shown.

- In **table 1**, some of the services seem on the boundary between categories: GAE (p43), for example, is described even in the formal GCP documentation sometimes as PaaS and sometimes as serverless. The table reflects my own judgement.
- In **table 2**, "both" is a curious category, which you'll understand better when we get to databases where nodes scale manually while shards scale automatically.

11

Table 1: types of GCP services

Infrastructure, including IaaS	<ul><li>GCE without MIG</li><li>GKE</li><li>Persistent disk</li><li>Local SSD</li><li>VPC</li><li>Deployment Manager</li></ul>
Managed service, including PaaS	<ul><li>GCE with MIG</li><li>GAE</li><li>Cloud Endpoints</li><li>Apigee Edge / Hybrid</li><li>Cloud Tasks</li><li>Istio / Anthos</li><li>GCS</li><li>Cloud SQL</li><li>Cloud Spanner</li><li>Cloud Bigtable</li><li>Firebase Realtime</li><li>Cloud Firestore/Datastore</li><li>Cloud Memorystore</li><li>Cloud Dataproc</li><li>Cloud Data Fusion</li><li>Cloud DNS</li><li>Cloud Router</li><li>Cloud NAT</li><li>Cloud Composer</li><li>Cloud Scheduler</li></ul>
Serverless	<ul><li>GCF</li><li>Cloud Run</li><li>BigQuery</li><li>Cloud Dataflow</li></ul>

Compute   Containers   Storage   Databases
Data services   Networking   Ops

12

Table 2: types of scaling on GCP

Always manual	Always auto	Manual or auto	Both
■ GCE without MIG ■ Persistent disk ■ Local SSD ■ Cloud Filestore ■ Cloud SQL ■ Cloud Memorystore ■ Cloud Data Fusion	■ GCF ■ Cloud Pub/Sub ■ Cloud Run ■ GCS ■ Cloud Firestore / Datastore ■ BigQuery ■ Cloud Dataprep ■ Cloud DNS ■ Cloud Router ■ Cloud NAT	■ GCE with MIG ■ GAE ■ Cloud Endpoints ■ GKE ■ Cloud Dataproc ■ Cloud Dataflow	■ Cloud Spanner ■ Cloud Bigtable

Compute   Containers   Storage   Databases   Data services   Networking

Chapter 2
GCP basics

2.1 Where is this cloud

Geography plays an important role in cloud architecture, because the location of your cloud resources is closely linked to your replication arrangements (p7) and also to the latency (p5) experienced by your users.

When you use GCP, you create resources on the Google global infrastructure. This infrastructure is divided into regions, and the regions are split into zones. Most GCP services are either global, regional or zonal, but sometimes this gets a bit more complex:

- **Zones**. GCP operates from 61 data centres around the world (I last checked in January 2020). Each one of them is a zone.
  - A zonal resource in one zone cannot be directly connected to a zonal resource in another zone.
  - Each zone is a different "failure domain". The data centres are isolated from each other, so there's a low risk that one problem will cause the failure of more than one zone.
  - To create **fault-tolerant** apps with **high availability**, you should deploy them in multiple zones.
  - If you deploy your app in a specific zone in order to serve it from a location close to your users, and this zone is unavailable so that the app is served from another zone, your users may experience higher latency. To minimise this impact, the standard practice is to choose multiple zones in the same region.
  - Some GCP services are only available in specific zones.

- **Regions**. The 61 zones are grouped into 20 regions.
  - Regional resources can be used by resources in all zones within the region.

- ▶ Regions are defined so that they are at least 100 miles apart from each other.
- ▶ Different regions are even less likely than zones to fail at the same time. So creating your resources in different regions provides higher availability and fault tolerance.
- ▶ Replicating your resources in multiple regions can further reduce latency, but this depends on where your users are.
- ▶ Some GCP services are only available in specific regions.

- **Global resources**. Global resources are accessible by resources in any zone in the same GCP project (p21).

- **Multi-regions**. GCP has 3 of these: Asia, Europe and US.
  - ▶ Resources with a multi-regional option can have built-in redundancy both within and across regions.

- **Dual-regions**. This option is similar to the multi-regional one but involves redundancy across exactly two regions.
  - ▶ This is offered for some resources in Europe and the US.

- **Network edge locations**. These are the 134 locations where Google's global private network connects to the internet.
  - ▶ They're also called Points of Presence or **POPs**.
  - ▶ The edge location where your traffic joins or leaves Google's network depends on your network tier (p144).
  - ▶ This is less related to which Google data centre hosts your resources, and more related to the location of your users.

- **CDN locations**. These are the 90 locations where GCP offers a CDN (p176) caching service.

- **Metros**. These are the 62 locations where you can create a Dedicated Interconnect (p173).
  - ▶ "Metro" stands for "metropolitan area", i.e. the city with a **colocation facility** that allows linking Google's network with your private network.
  - ▶ You'd typically choose a metro close to your on-prem network, to reduce latency.
  - ▶ Each metro supports a subset of GCP regions.

15

▶ Each metro is split into at least two zones called **edge availability domains**. These domains go through maintenance at different times, so that your Interconnect remains active also during maintenance.

Table 3 shows the geographical scope of different GCP services. When the table shows more than one scope for the same GCP service, it means that you can choose. The text colours indicate which chapter in this book describes each service.

It is also worth noting that:

- Questions in your certification exam will definitely require knowledge of the geographical scope of common GCP services.
- Redundancy across zones, regions or both is a common **disaster recovery** (**DR**) plan. If your resources are stored in multiple places then they are more likely to survive a disaster. This likelihood further increases if these different places are far from each other, i.e. in different regions.
- Redundancy is not the only DR approach. For example, you may keep a resource in one zone only but also store a snapshot (p70) of it, or any other form of backup, in a different zone or region.
- Various terms with the word "zone" are used by Cloud DNS (p163). This is a different meaning of the word "zone", not directly related to the location of GCP resources.
- Some GCP-related services are offered by third-party providers. This includes, for example, Partner Interconnect (p174), CDN Interconnect (p177) and Carrier Peering (p176). The locations where these services are offered are not included in **table 3**.

Table 3: the geography of GCP services

Resource	Global	Multi-regional	Dual-regional	Regional	Zonal	At edge locations	At CDN locations	At metros
GCE disk image	■							
GCE instance template	■							
Cloud Pub/Sub	■							
All proxy load balancers	■							
Cloud Interconnect	■							
VPC network & routes	■							
Firewall	■							
Cloud DNS	■							
IP address	■			■				
Cloud KMS	■	■	■	■				
GCS		■	■	■				
Disk snapshots		■		■				
Cloud Spanner		■		■				
Cloud Bigtable		■		■				
Firestore/Datastore		■		■				
BigQuery		■		■				

17

Resource	Global	Multi-regional	Dual-regional	Regional	Zonal	At edge locations	At CDN locations	At metros
GAE				■				
GCF				■				
Cloud Tasks				■				
Cloud SQL				■				
Firebase Realtime				■				
Cloud Memorystore				■				
Network load balancer				■				
Internal load balancers				■				
Interconnect attachment				■				
VPC subnet				■				
Cloud NAT				■				
Cloud Router				■				
Cloud VPN				■				
MIG				■	■			
Persistent disk				■	■			
Cloud Dataflow				■	■			

Resource	Global	Multi-regional	Dual-regional	Regional	Zonal	At edge locations	At CDN locations	At metros
GKE cluster				■	■			
Cloud Dataproc				■	■			
GCE instance					■			
Cloud Filestore					■			
NEG					■			
Cloud composer					■			
Data ingress/egress based on network tier						■		
Cloud CDN							■	
Cloud Interconnect								■

Compute   *Containers*   *Storage*   *Databases*
Data services   *Networking*   **Security**   *Operations*

2.2 Your GCP resources

GCP have **quotas** for your cloud resources.

- For each kind of GCP service, the quotas define the maximum you can create or use, if the resources are available.
- Quotas don't guarantee availability of the GCP service you want. They exist for other reasons, like preventing unexpected levels of traffic.
- Some quota restrictions are global – for example, for load balancers, firewalls and VPNs.

- Some quota restrictions are regional – for example, for CPUs, GPUs and disks.
- When the resource is zonal, quotas are usually regional, for example in the case of GCE instances. However, there might be limited availability in your preferred zone.
- Some GCP resources, such as IPs, have quota restrictions both regionally and globally.
- If you are restricted by quotas, you can contact Google and request that they change your limits.
- The exam may present situations where one architecture option looks reasonable but it exceeds the quotas, for example in the questions about the published case studies (p216).
- You are not expected to memorise quota restrictions. In this book I've included quota examples for specific services, GCS and BigQuery, because this is where I've found that hitting the quotas in your actual work is most likely.

Many GCP services offer a **service level agreement** (**SLA**). Note that:
- Newer services sometimes don't have an SLA, or they only offer a limited one.
- SLA details evolve constantly, so in this book I only mention those which attract most attention, such as the SLA for GCS durability and availability (p76).
- An SLA includes a list of service level indicators (**SLI**).
- An SLI has guaranteed service level objectives (**SLO**) and some info on what you should expect if SLOs are not met.
- SLAs are a common thing in IT, but the concept of SLIs and SLOs is part of Google's **Site Reliability Engineering** (**SRE**) methodology.

The resources you create in GCP are organised in a hierarchy. There are also some non-hierarchical ways to group or categorise your resources. **Table 4** gives an overview of all of these.

Table 4: grouping and categorising resources

Concept	When you apply it	What does it categorise	How to make the most of it
Orgs (p2)	Before you create any resources	The org is the root of the hierarchy of your GCP resources.	Place resources in different orgs only if you want to isolate them from each other.
Folders	Before you create any resources	Split your org into folders that you can place projects in.	Set IAM policies per folder, so that different projects share common policies.
Projects	Before adding resources that need to be billed separately, or separated from each other in other ways	Every resource belongs to one project. It's similar to an "account" in AWS (p5). Resources in the same project can communicate with each other regularly.	Use projects to represent real projects or other collections of resources. Create templates to automate project creation, e.g. with Cloud Deployment Manager.
Labels	When you create compute, storage and networking resources	Each label is a key-value pair you attach to resources to indicate things like: ■ Team name ■ Cost centre ■ Solution name ■ Env (e.g. test) ■ State (e.g. archive)	Filter resources by label to track usage or spend. Break down your bill by label.

21

Concept	When you apply it	What does it categorise	How to make the most of it
Network tags	When setting up GCE instances inside a specific VPC	You attach tags to instances in order to: ■ Determine the source and destination of firewall rules. ■ Attach network routes to VMs.	Control traffic within a VPC.
Security marks	When setting up Cloud Security Command Centre	Marks are similar to labels, but: ■ IAM permissions apply to the marks themselves. ■ Marks can be based on labels and tags.	Perform security analysis if you're in a suitable IAM role.
Resource groups	When setting up Cloud Monitoring	■ Group membership is automated based on criteria – e.g. all resources in a region. ■ Resources can belong to multiple groups.	Do separate monitoring for each resource group. Create subgroups if needed (up to six depth levels are allowed).
Instance groups	When setting up GCE instances	It lets you manage multiple identical VMs as a single entity.	Use auto-scaling or load balancing across VMs.

22

Concept	When you apply it	What does it categorise	How to make the most of it
Selector labels	When setting up GKE	It lets you group GKE resources, for example to define which pods run a single service.	Use micro-services as part of a loosely-coupled solution architecture.
Buckets	When adding objects to GCS	You group objects into buckets and can apply settings either to entire buckets or to individual objects.	Apply storage classes, permissions and policies by bucket.
Sub-accounts	With the billing API	You split projects into different subaccounts so that they are shown separately in your bill.	Use it if you are a reseller, and each of your GCP projects is billed to a different customer.
Roles	Whenever you define or change IAM permissions	Each role is a collection of all permissions required for a certain type of user.	Never give permissions to people directly. Give people a pre-defined role instead.
Key rings	When managing security keys in KMS	Security keys in the same project and location can by in one key ring.	Give permissions to a key ring if all keys in it need these permission.

Compute   Containers   Storage   Networking   Security   Ops

23

The GCP hierarchy puts resources inside projects; projects inside folders; and folders inside orgs. You use the **Resource Manager** to manage this hierarchical structure and the way resources can be accessed. Using the Resource Manager is free (you pay for the resources, not for the manager!).

An important use of the Resource Manager is for managing **org policies**. You should know that:
- Wherever the org hierarchy splits into different branches, there is a "node". Wherever this a node, you can define an org policy for all resources that branch from that node.
- The org policy defines constraints on how resources are used. Each constraint is a specific restriction on specific GCP services.
- By default, an org policy applies for all descendants of the node it was set for. Each node inherits the org policies from the nodes higher in the hierarchy.
- The union of all org policies that apply to a resource will determine how it can be used. It's your responsibility to set policies so that this union has the desired effect. Also, new org policies don't apply retroactively, so you need to plan how to avoid policy conflict.
- Org policies are different from IAM policies: an IAM policy assigns roles to members (p178). An org is somewhat similar to a role, since both of these define permissions. But an org policy is applied to a resource, not to a member.

Another GCP service that helps manage your resources is the **Cloud Asset Inventory**. Things you should know:
- This is a time series database, containing the last-five-weeks history of your asset inventory, including asset metadata.
- The assets in this inventory include all your GCP resources, but the definition of "assets" also includes org policies, IAM policies (p179), and VPC service controls (p192).
- With the inventory, you can look at an "asset snapshot", i.e. the set of assets that an org, folder or project had at a specific time point.

24

- You can export a snapshot or the history of asset change events.

Each org in GCP is linked to a **domain**:
- The domain is not another level in the resource hierarchy, because there is exactly one org per domain.
- The importance of the domain is that it connects your org to resources which are defined using Google services outside GCP: either G Suite (p32) or Cloud Identity (p183).
- You often use G Suite or Cloud Identity to define users, groups (of users), and devices. By sharing a domain with your GCP org, these resources can use the same identity and access control policies across different Google services.

Each project in GCP is linked to a **billing account**:
- Each billing account gets one invoice in one currency.
- The billing account is a GCP resource, but the actual payment is handled outside GCP. This is done by connecting the billing account to a **Google payment profile**.
- The billing account defines who pays; the payment profile defines how they pay.
- Different GCP projects can connect to the same billing account or to different ones. Different billing accounts can connect to the same payment profile or to different ones.
- There are two types of billing accounts. An **invoiced** account is billed monthly and paid by cheque or transfer. A **self-serve** account can be billed either monthly or when it has accrued an agreed amount; it is paid automatically by card or direct debit.
- There are two types of payments profiles: individual (with no allowance for multiple users) or business.
- A **subaccount** is a billing account for resellers:
  - ▶ Subaccounts are part of a master billing account, which must be on invoiced billing.
  - ▶ The reseller can group together the projects they resell to the same customer, and then these form a separate section in the invoice, with its own subtotal.
  - ▶ With the **Cloud Billing APIs** you can automate the creation and management of subaccounts, to fit it into your reselling process.
- Recommended practices for billing –

- ▶ Plan your costs using the GCP online **calculator**.
- ▶ Set **budgets** in advance for your billing account, your projects or both.
- ▶ Set **alerts** to warn you when your spending on GCP reaches certain budget thresholds.
- ▶ Note that budgets don't limit spending, they just generate alerts. But you can also use **quotas** to cap the consumption of a particular resource.
- ▶ Export your bills to BigQuery (p108) to analyse your cost breakdown.
- ▶ Use the **Cloud Billing APIs** to automate all the above.

Since we're talking about billing, you should also look at table 8 later in this book (p86). Although I've put it in another chapter, it is highly relevant here, since it splits your GCP costs into those you need to commit to in advance and those you don't.

2.3 Accessing your resources

Since this book is about architecture, I won't focus on how you implement your GCP solutions in detail. There's relatively little in this book about your hands-on interaction with GCP. However, there are some facts about this interaction which architects should know well, because:

- These facts apply to almost every GCP service.
- You might need them during the architecture design stage.
- They ask about them in the exam.

So in this section I review the basics of how you access GCP in order to create, configure, programme and manage the resources you include in your solution. You should consider the content of this section as if I repeated it in every chapter of this book, because it is relevant to anything you do with GCP.

The main ways to access your GCP resources are summarised in **table 5**.

Table 5: ways to interact with GCP

Method	What is it	What it's for
Console	An online UI to access on your browser	■ Experimenting with resource types you don't know well, so you want to view default settings or choose options from drop-down lists ■ Performing actions using wizards, structured forms and help menus ■ Any one-off task you want to do manually
APIs	Dozens of APIs covering most capabilities of most GCP services	■ Writing code to create, configure and update GCP resources by direct use of the HTTP protocol ■ Using this code as part of automated or scheduled processes ■ Using this code interactively with a web proxy tool ■ GCP APIs have versions using the universal **REST** conventions and alternative versions using Google's lightweight **gRPC** approach
Client libraries	A set of "wrappers" for the APIs	■ Accessing the same APIs via code in your preferred programming language instead of direct HTTP
CLI	A set of interactive tools covering most capabilities of most GCP services	■ Using CLI tools interactively once you install the GCP software development kit (**SDK**) ■ Using CLI tools interactively via the **Cloud Shell** in your browser ■ Writing scripts to create, configure and update GCP resources from a command line ■ Using these scripts as part of automated or scheduled processes

To use GCP APIs directly, you first need to sort out a few things:
- You need to enable the API. This adds different capabilities to your GCP project (p21), depending on the service you've enabled. It may add monitoring pages to your GCP console, turn billing on, and makes relevant IAM roles (p179) visible.
- Some APIs are enabled by default (e.g. GCS, BigQuery, Cloud Datastore, Cloud SQL, Ops Suite). Others are not.
- Some APIs (e.g. GCE) can be enabled simply by navigating to the page of the relevant service on the GCP console.
- In other cases, APIs are enabled on the "API Library" page in the console or with the "*gcloud services enable*" CLI command.
- An app that makes calls to GCP APIs needs to be registered. In the registration process, you get credentials that the app can then use when making API calls.
- To authenticate to GCP APIs you should use service accounts (p181) or methods like OAuth2 (p9). Specific APIs also accept simple API keys, especially APIs you often call from front end apps without a backend (p8). API keys are not recommended because they don't identify who's making the request.

Generally, the first three of the four GCP access methods listed in table 5 follow fairly universal concepts. You may have seen other cases where a service is accessed remotely via a web UI, API or client library. The CLI is not a unique concept either, but the way it works with the different GCP services is not obvious.

The following are different CLI tools which are commonly used for work with GCP:
- **gcloud** is for most GCP services
- **kubectl** is for GKE (p52)
- **gsutil** is for GCS (p73)
- **bq** is for BigQuery (p108)
- **cbt** is for Cloud Bigtable (p102)

You can use these tools if you've installed the SDK on your system or if you are working with the Cloud Shell in the browser. We'll talk about gsutil, bq, cbt and kubectl in later chapters. I don't know why BigQuery has its own CLI tool while Cloud

Spanner, for example, works with gcloud. I assume the logic behind the set of CLIs will continue to evolve in the future.

With **gcloud**, a typical statement starts with "*gcloud*", followed by the name of the GCP service you want to work with, followed by more specific actions, parameters and/or flags. Unhelpfully, the name of the GCP service used with gcloud doesn't always match the name used elsewhere. But if you're an architect then you'd typically search for the exact syntax you need whenever you need it, rather than memorise any of it.

Below are some examples. I use them here to illustrate the general use of gcloud, not to get into any detailed syntax.

- *gcloud compute instances list* (to list your GCE instances)
- *gcloud compute instances list --filter="name ~ ^my-.*"* (to list GCE instances and apply a filter to the list)
- *gcloud compute copy-files example-instance:~/folder-cloud ~/folder-local --zone asia-southeast1-c* (to download a file)
- *gcloud compute instances create vm1 --image image-1 --tags test --zone us-central1-a --machine-type f1-micro* (to create a VM of a specific machine type, using a specific disk image, with a specific tag, in a specific zone)
- *gcloud compute instances attach-disk my-cool-instance –my-cool-disk* (to attach a persistent disk to a GCE instance)
- *gcloud compute networks subnets create subnet1 --network net1 --range 10.5.5.0/24* (to create a VPC subnet)
- *gcloud dns record-sets list --zone europe-west4-b* (to list DNS records)
- *gcloud compute firewall-rules create the-best-rule --network default --allow tcp:9200 tcp:3306* (to create a firewall rule)
- *gcloud sql instances list* (to list Cloud SQL instances)
- *gcloud auth list* (to list accounts whose credentials are stored on the local system)
- *gcloud builds submit --config=cloudbuild.yaml* (to submit a build file)

Two important gcloud features are **gcloud config** and **gcloud init**. Whatever you do with the CLI uses a configuration which applies to your statements even if you don't type it each time.

This config defines the account you use, and therefore it relates to who you are and what permissions you have. With gcloud config you manage these configs; with gcloud init you can start doing some work based on a default config.

When you use Cloud Shell, you automatically get access to an ephemeral (p10) Linux VM that runs while your session is live, and to a "*$HOME*" folder with 5 GB of storage that persists beyond your session. Not only the GCP CLI tools are pre-installed in the Shell, but also other common tools such as vim, make, maven, pip, common programming languages, MySQL client, Docker client, and whatnot. An optional "boost mode" in the Cloud Shell gives you a more powerful VM.

2.4 GCP brands

Some of the core GCP services have names that start with the words "Google Cloud" or "Cloud". There are specific services, like BigQuery, which don't follow this pattern but Google are clear enough that these services are a central part of GCP.

But some services that come with GCP are branded differently, and it's not too clear if Google see them as equal members of the GCP family. I review this range of brands in this section in an attempt to reduce the confusion, despite this lack of clarity.

My recommendation is that you become broadly familiar with all of these services before you take a GCP exam. This will surely make you wiser even if much of this info ends up out of scope!

- **Firebase**. This is a platform for web and mobile app development. It includes some cloud services that overlap in their scope with GCP services. Firebase was acquired by Google in 2014 but continues to sell its own products under its own brand. They maintain separate consoles, APIs and pricing plans. To further complicate things -
    - ▶ The GCP Cloud Datastore (p106) service is being gradually dissolved into the Firebase Firestore. At the moment Google use four different service names: Cloud Datastore,

30

Cloud Firestore, Cloud Firestore in Datastore Mode, and Cloud Firestore in Native Mode.
   ▶ GCS for Firebase (p82) is a service for Firebase customers that uses GCS infrastructure under the hood.
   ▶ GCP documentation presents specific Firebase services, like Firebase Authentication (p186) and Firebase Test Lab (p207), as the native GCP solution for specific use cases.
- **Apigee**. This is another platform that was acquired by Google and partially embedded into GCP. Some Apigee products for API management (p46) are listed as integral GCP services, but they retain a separate branding within GCP. Their integration with the wider set of GCP services (e.g. GCS or BigQuery) uses Apigee Extensions, which are available with some Apigee customer plans but not all. Some integration features between Apigee and GCP are still in Beta.
- **Completed acquisitions**. Some technologies acquired by Google now only live on GCP. Examples include –
   ▶ The former Velostrata migration tool is now only available as Migrate for Compute Engine (p41), and the former name is no longer in use.
   ▶ The Zync rending service (p142) is part of GCP but keeps its independent brand.
- **Trifacta**. This is a separate company, not owned by Google, with its own products. One of them is embedded into GCP under the name Cloud Dataprep by Trifacta (p119) while other versions of the same service are also available outside GCP.
- **Open-source Google services**. Some popular open-source projects originally started as Google projects, and they now live a double life both as a managed GCP service and as an open-source technology –
   ▶ An important example is Kubernetes (p51) and its ecosystem of supporting services such as Knative (p64). There are now two parallel ecosystems based on these, one within GCP and one outside, with quite a complex relationship between the two.
   ▶ Another example is Cloud Dataflow (p125) in GCP, with its open-source sibling Apache Beam (p124).
- **GCP implementations of open-source tools**. Some GCP services have an open-source technology at their heart –

31

- ▶ The Ops Suite (p203) implements Fluentd for log analysis and Collectd for performance monitoring.
- ▶ Cloud Memorystore (p113) is based on Redis for caching.
- ▶ Cloud Composer (p203) is based on Apache Airflow for workflow management.
- ▶ Several GCP services (from BigQuery to Cloud Formation Toolkit) have features that welcome integration with Terraform for writing "infrastructure as code".

- **Open-source contribution to GCP**. The Forseti (p196) security tools are open-source and community-driven, although they are tailor-made for GCP.
- **Mix of Google brands**. Google sometimes encourage GCP users to use other Google products such as G Suite, which is the Google equivalent of Microsoft 365. The way you are encouraged to do so can take different forms –
  - ▶ The users of your GCP-based solutions sometimes need to be added as G Suite users, so that they can have the same identity in GCP and in services like Google Docs, Google Drive or Google Calendar.
  - ▶ GCP documentation covers situations where it may be better to use the G Suite Direct Peering (p175) instead of the GCP Cloud Interconnect (p172).
  - ▶ Connected sheets (p119) is an example of a G Suite feature based on a GCP service.
  - ▶ Google's BeyondCorp branding of its corporate security support is sometimes used when describing the need for some GCP services.
- **Sub-brands within GCP**. Some groups of GCP services have their own mini-brand, like AutoML (p133) (and till recently also Stackdriver).
- **GCP Marketplace**. Many other technologies from various providers are offered to GCP users on the GCP Marketplace (p215). Unlike other items on the list above, a product cannot be seen as an integral GCP service just because it is in the GCP Marketplace. However, the Marketplace itself is an important GCP service.

Chapter 3
Compute services

3.1 Google Computer Engine

You use the **Google Compute Engine** (**GCE**) to create VMs (p6) in GCP. You use GCE if you want to manage servers the way you do on-prem, but without having to maintain the hardware itself.

- Each VM is a GCE instance. It is created in a specific zone and belongs to a specific VPC network (p144).
- When creating a VM you pick a **machine type** and boot disk image. **Table 6** shows the main categories of machine types. There are many machine sub-types in each category; the table only summarises some high-level info.
- Each VM has a boot disk that contains the operating system. Your create the boot disk from an image, which you choose based on the operating system you want.
- The boot disk image can be your own **custom image**, or a **public** one (from Google or from any other source).
- There are many boot disk image options, split into "families" such as Windows images, Linux images, SQL Server, "container-optimised" (with Docker installed), and so on.
- The "family" makes it easy to identify the latest version.
- A custom image can be based on any of these:
    - ▶ Another image in your project.
    - ▶ An image shared from another project.
    - ▶ A compressed image in GCS (p73).
    - ▶ A persistent disk (p70).
    - ▶ A snapshot of a persistent disk (p70).
- It's worth highlighting that images exist in order to create boot disks. Snapshots can be used for this too, but this is not their main purpose; the main role of snapshots is for backup.
- An image needs to include a **driver** for the interface that connects the VM to a disk. Without a matching pair (a driver and a disk interface), disk speeds will be reduced.
- In addition to the boot disk, you usually also attach a persistent disk (p70) to every VM for file storage.
- When creating a VM, you can also add labels (p21) to it.

33

Table 6: machine types

Type	What it's for	Things to know
N1	Classical "general purpose" machines	■ Up to 96 vCPUs. ■ Memory per vCPU – 1 GB to 6.5 GB. ■ Largest sustained use discount (p37). ■ Pre-defined sub-types in this family include standard machines, high-memory machines, high-CPU machines. ■ Custom types available, based on your own specification. ■ Local SSD (p71) available. ■ GPUs (p3) available only with this type!
N2	"Next generation" general purpose machines with better performance	■ Up to 80 vCPUs. ■ Memory per vCPU – 0.5 GB to 8 GB, or more with "extended memory" option. ■ Higher clock frequency. ■ Pre-defined sub-types similar to N1. ■ Custom types available. ■ Local SSD available.
E2	"Cost optimised" general purpose, currently in Beta	■ Up to 16 vCPUs. ■ Memory per vCPU – 8 GB to 128 GB. ■ Sub-types: micro, small, medium, standard, high memory, high CPU. ■ Custom types available.
M1/ M2	"Memory optimised" for large in-memory storage	■ Up to 400 vCPUs. ■ Memory per vCPU up to 28 GB. ■ Can reach 12 TB memory. ■ No regional persistent disks (p70). ■ Sub-types: ultra, mega.

Type	What it's for	Things to know
C2	Compute-intensive, for games, single-thread apps and other intense loads	■ Latest Intel Scalable Cascade Lake Processors. ■ Up to 60 vCPUs. ■ Can reach 240 GB memory. ■ No regional persistent disks (p70). ■ Local SSD available.
F1/ G2	Shared core machines, for apps with modest needs	■ You get access to one vCPU that only runs 20% of the time (f1-micro sub-type) or 50% (g1-small sub-type). ■ These machines offer bursting capabilities, using additional CPU for short periods of time.

■ You can (optionally) choose an instance **template** that already has the machine type, boot disk image, labels and other config detail already defined.

3.2 Managing your VMs

It is critical to note that GCE is not a managed service. What you do with your instances is your own business. This section lists GCE instance management features you need to know.

■ When you create an instance using a public image from Google, a "guest environment" is installed by default, with a set of processes that GCP needs in order to keep your VM infrastructure running.
■ If you use a custom image, you install the guest env manually.
■ GCE offers "live migration" to keep your VMs running during maintenance or failure. At such times, it migrates your VM to another host (p6) in the same zone and doesn't need a reboot.
■ To configure any apps on your instances, you can SSH (p9) into the machine if you use Linux, or RDP if you use Windows.
■ Cloud Audit Logs (p209) create for you logs of resource changes ("admin activity logs") and system maintenance ops ("system event logs").

35

- There's no automated logging of other read/write ops ("data access logs") or any activity inside your VMs. If you want to, you can add the logging agent (p210) app.
- Similarly, Cloud Monitoring (p211) examines the behaviour of your VM from the outside, excluding metrics of what happens inside. For more specific monitoring, use the monitoring agent (p211), or use managed compute services instead GCE.
- **Managed instance groups (MIGs)** are a key part of GCE:
  - ▶ A MIG contains identical VMs that you manage as a single entity, either in one zone (**zonal MIG**) or across zones in one region (**regional MIG**).
  - ▶ MIGs are the way for GCE to auto-scale. Although they also do other nice things, MIGs are primarily the GCE auto-scaling solution.
  - ▶ MIGs offer a degree of load balancing even if you don't use a load balancer (p156). Work or requests that get sent to a MIG are distributed so that healthy instances share the load evenly, more or less.
  - ▶ Other managed features that MIGs give to your VMs: high availability, health checking, rolling updates, auto-healing.
  - ▶ MIGs are good for **stateless** servers, i.e. servers that don't need to store info locally in one session ("state") to use later. The later session will probably be served by a different instance in the group, so the MIG approach isn't good for **stateful** apps.
  - ▶ MIG are also suitable for batch work, that gets allocated to instances by a queue of things to do. The queue itself isn't provided by the MIG, only the VMs that can do the work.
  - ▶ Each VM in a MIG is created from an instance **template**.
  - ▶ **Auto-scaling policies** can be configured to specify how you want the group to scale and what should trigger it (CPU utilisation, load balancing capacity, Cloud Monitoring metrics, or queue-based workload).
- **Unmanaged instance groups** are distant cousins of MIGs. They can have a role in load balancing, but they have none of the other MIG features.
- When a GCE instance is running, it has an identity that determines what it is allowed to do.

- ▶ The instance identity is provided by a **service account** (p181). You need to create the service account in the same GCP project before you create the instance.
- ▶ If, for example, an app that runs in your VM needs to write files to GCS, then the service account needs the relevant GCS permissions.
- ▶ In addition to the service account, you also define the **access scopes** of your instance. There are many access scopes to choose from; they limit what your instance can do even if the service account has wider permissions.
- ▶ However, access scopes are a legacy method; they don't add much security. They work well with OAuth2 (p9) requests, like those you make with gcloud and client libraries, but not with other authentication methods, like those used by gRPC (p27). It's best to give the instance the full "cloud-platform" access scope and limit its permissions via the roles (p179) of the service account.
- ▶ Sometimes you may want to verify the identity of a VM, for example when sending credentials to it. An app can verify instance identity using a unique JWT (p9), signed by Google's OAuth2 (p9) certificate. The GCE metadata server will generate this token if the instance itself requests it.

3.3 Paying for your VMs

Making wise use of GCE has a lot to do with learning its approach to pricing and different types of discounts:
- Generally, you pay for every second a VM is running (1 minute minimum), based on the machine type, and also for every GB of network traffic if data leaves the zone where your VM is.
- Payment for disks and images is separate from VM use.
- Prices for different machine types are "resource-based", which means that each vCPU (p6) and each GB of memory is billed separately, whether or not they're of the same machine type.
- There are 3 important types of discount, based on either sustained use, committed use, or use of preemptible VMs.
- **Sustained use discount** applies to GCE resources that you use more than 25% of the time during any month.
  - ▶ Once you've used your vCPUs and GBs of memory this much, you get this discount for every additional second.

- ▶ The discount itself increases with usage, up to 30% net discount for resources that run the entire month.
- ▶ The discount applies to all your resource usage in a region collectively, but it's separate in each region.
- ▶ The discount is calculated separately for each family of machine types – predefined, custom, memory-optimised, compute-optimised, shared core.
- **Committed use discounts** applies if you buy a 1-year or 3-year "commitment" for a specific machine type.
  - ▶ Most machine types can get up to 57% discount.
  - ▶ Memory-optimised machines can get up to 70% discount.
  - ▶ A committed use discount doesn't reserve capacity in a specific zone. You need make a **reservation** separately.
- **Preemptible** instances are VMs you can use at a lower price but without guarantee that they'll remain available.
  - ▶ GCE might terminate your preemptible machines if the resources are needed elsewhere.
  - ▶ Preemptible instances last up to 24 hours.
  - ▶ You can create preemptible instances in a MIG and use them for batch cluster jobs: if some instances terminate, the process slows down but doesn't stop.
  - ▶ If GCE needs to terminate a VM, it sends a preemption notice first. You can use a shutdown script to take clean-up actions before the instance stops.
  - ▶ Preempted instances will still appear in your project, but in a "terminated" state that is not charged. You can recover data from persistent disks attached to these instances.
  - ▶ If you use AWS (p5), you'll know the similar concept of "spot" instances. Unlike AWS "spot" instances, getting preemptible ones doesn't involve bidding.
- Alongside these discounts there are also some premium GCE services. An important one is the use of **sole-tenant nodes**. These are physical servers hosting only VMs for a specific project. You pay a 10% sole-tenancy premium.
- Various quotas apply to your instances, both regional and global. They apply even if an instance isn't running. You can choose to separate your preemptible quotas from the quotas for your other machines.

3.4 More about your VMs

Every instance stores its **metadata** on a metadata server.
- The metadata includes host name, instance ID, service account, and "custom metadata".
- SSH keys, startup scripts and shutdown scripts are all stored as custom metadata.
- Custom metadata is limited to 256 KB per individual entry, or 512 KB of total metadata per instance. Startup and shutdown scripts often exceed this, so you can store them on GCS and include just a URL in the metadata.
- You can send metadata queries to the metadata URL (metadata.google.internal) or use tools like curl or wget, from within the instance.
- Some metadata entries (like "attributes/") are folders that contain other metadata keys.
- "Guest attributes" are a type of metadata parameters that can contain small pieces of info that require infrequent access (up to 10 queries / minute), for example to ensure a startup script configures apps correctly.

An instance can be in one of the following **states**:
- Provisioning (while space for the VM is found and reserved)
- Staging (while preparing the host and network)
- Running (as soon as the operating system starts booting up)
- Stopping (a temporary state due to failure or manual stop)
- Terminated (after the VM fails or stopped manually)
- Repairing (after finding an internal error).

Startup scripts perform tasks every time your instance boots up. **Shutdown scripts** execute commands right before an instance is terminated or restarted.
- Startup and shutdown scripts are especially useful for instances in a MIG with auto-scaling, because such instances need to start and finish their work without your manual help.
- Scripts can be in any language that the VM understands. I recommend that you avoid Yiddish, only my mum gets it.
- Startup scripts run when the network is available. Use them to install software, perform updates or turn on services.

- Shutdown actions may include cleaning up, exporting logs, copying data to GCS, or syncing with other systems.
- Shutdown scripts have a limited time to run before the VM stops. It's usually 90 seconds, or just 30 after preemption of preemptible instances. It's your responsibility to design your instances and scripts so that they complete on time.
- Scripts run with the "root" identity.

3.5 Right-sizing

GCP has two new tools that can give you recommendations about your GCE instances. The first of these is the **instance sizing recommender**:

- It suggests changes to your GCE machine types, to optimise memory utilisation and/or the number of vCPUs.
- It can estimate the cost difference between the current and recommended instance sizes.
- The recommendations are based on data collected in 60-second intervals over the last 8 days. So if your workload follows weekly patterns then the recommender would pick this up. It is less suitable if you have spikes that are either infrequent or shorter than a minute.
- Sizing recommendations are not yet available for VMs instances created using GAE flex (p44), Cloud Dataflow (p125) or GKE (p52). They are also not available for VMs with local SSD disks (p71), GPUs (p3) or TPUs (p50).

Another tool is the **MIG sizing recommender**:

- It helps you choose the best machine type for your MIG (p36), to optimise the utilisation of your instances.
- Note that despite that name "MIG sizing", this is not about choosing the size of the MIG!
- Here, too, the recommendations are based on data collected in 60-second intervals over the last 8 days.
- Recommendations are available for single-zone MIGs that are neither auto-scaled nor load-balanced.
- You only get recommendations for machine types that are available in the zone where the instance is running.

- Typical cases where such recommendations help:
  - ▶ When your workloads have periodic or seasonal changes in traffic.
  - ▶ When you have to keep the number of instances constant for licensing reasons but can flex the machine type.
  - ▶ When the processes you run aren't suitable for auto-scaling.
- Cases where these recommendations are less helpful:
  - ▶ If your CPU spikes are very short.
  - ▶ If your spikes happen less often than once in 8 days.
  - ▶ If you deliberately under-utilise your MIG, for example for licensing reasons or just to be on the safe side.
  - ▶ If CPU doesn't affect your machine type preference.
- The recommendation lists actions related to your instance template, and separate actions related to the MIG manager.

3.6 Migrating on-prem VMs to GCE

Here are two tools for migration (p4) you should be aware of.

- The **virtual disk import tool** is your friend if you have "golden disks" with software and config that you want to replicate in GCE.
  - ▶ The tool helps you import these disks and images so that you can create instances from them.
  - ▶ It supports virtual disk file formats like VMDK and VHD.
- **Migrate for Compute Engine** is a service for migrating VMs from VMware vSphere, AWS EC2, Azure VMs or physical servers.
  - ▶ This tool has two different offers: "running a VM in GCP", where storage remains on-prem and is just cached (p5) on GCP, or "migrating a VM to GCP", which creates native GCP disks.
  - ▶ The idea behind these two offers is that you can run the VM in GCP while storage is being migrated, and detach the on-prem VM later, to reduce migration risk.
  - ▶ In line with these two offers, disk changes made on GCE can be either be in "write back mode" or in "isolation mode". The former (only from vSphere VMs) sends the changes back to the on-prem disk; the latter doesn't.

▶ Components of Migrate for Compute Engine include "Cloud Extensions" (to handle storage migration) and "Exporter" (to create persistent disks when detaching on-prem disks).
▶ To perform a large migration, you need to divide it into "sprints" with one or more "waves" per sprint. For each wave you define "runbooks" and "jobs". A runbook is a CSV file that specifies the source and target VMs. A job is the migration operation on the list of VMs in the runbook.
▶ It requires inbound iSCSI access from the on-prem VMs to GCP; iSCSI is the network protocol that allows connecting a computer to remote storage as if it was a local disk.
▶ The tool is free; you pay for the GCP services you use after the migration.

3.7 Google Cloud Functions

Google Cloud Functions (**GCF**) is a very important service; don't be misled by how short this section is. GCF takes care of so much of your work, compared to GCE for example, that there's simply less to write about it.

- If GCE offers you IaaS (p6) then GCF offers FaaS, that is **function as a service**.
- It is a serverless (p7) product, so you only need to develop the function you want to deploy. The servers that your functions run on are provisioned, maintained, auto-scaled and load-balanced by GCP.
- You only pay for these servers when they are in use. You pay for the CPU and memory allocated to your function, only for the time the function runs, in units of 100ms.
- The functions run code which can be written using Node.js, Python or Go.
- GCF is event-driven (p10). You decide what counts as an event. Events can occur in any system, so long as you can make them trigger a GCF request once an event has occurred.
- Your functions only run when such requests arrive.
- Every function gets an HTTP endpoint (p5), so you don't need to set up an API. An IP address is automatically assigned to

your endpoint. If you must have a static IP address for a function, then GCF isn't the right solution for you.
- Some GCP services have built-in events defined so that they can trigger GCF requests easily. For example, a new object stored on GCS can generate a GCF call, and you can also subscribe a function to a Cloud Pub/Sub topic (p47).
- GCF is regional. It runs in all zones in your selected region.
- GCF authenticates requests but doesn't filter outbound traffic. This violates a PCI DSS requirement for companies of SAQ type A-EP and D (p199). If this applies to you, you need to have "compensating controls" in place to mitigate the risk, or use other services like GCE or GKE instead.

3.8 Google App Engine

The Google App Engine (GAE) is a managed service you can use to host web apps.
- Your app can run on GAE if your code can be organised as a single resource. So GAE isn't suitable for hosting systems with complex external dependencies.
- However, if this constraint is met, GAE can be powerful, since a GAE app can run multiple services. It can host a set of micro-services (p4), either related to each other or not.
- Using GAE means that GCP takes care of most of your server-side needs, including patching, health checking and so on.
- Each service you include in your app has one or more versions. You can use different versions, even at the same time, for rollback, testing, or a phased release. You can give GAE rules for how to split traffic between releases.
- There are two different GAE products, the **Standard Environment** ("GAE Standard") and the **Flexible Env** ("GAE Flex"). The Standard Env is actually not so standard, and the Flex one is not necessarily more flexible! They are just two different PaaS options (p6) for serving apps.
- Here's how **GAE Standard** works -
  - ▶ It runs your apps in "sandbox" instances, which are like booths within a larger VM, each sandbox doing nothing else but running your app.
  - ▶ You choose an instance class, which determines the compute resources (vCPU, memory) and pricing.

- ▶ GAE Standard can run apps programmed in Python, Java, Node.js, PHP, Ruby or Go.
- ▶ It has the cool feature of **auto-scaling-to-zero**, which means you pay nothing when there's no demand, because no instance is running. In this sense, GAE Standard is as serverless as GCF (p42).
- ▶ It can also scale up very quickly to a high number of instances if your app experiences extreme demand spikes.
- ▶ You can select manual scaling instead.
- ▶ GAE sends to Cloud Logging (p208) logs of the requests made to your app and of some of the app activity.

- Here's how **GAE Flex** works -
  - ▶ It runs your apps in Docker containers (p51) hosted on GCE instances.
  - ▶ It has the known benefits of Docker apps, such as your freedom to carefully optimise the specification of your containers for your needs.
  - ▶ It offers auto-scaling, but it is less suitable for extreme and sudden variations in traffic than GAE Standard. Scaling down in GAE Flex doesn't go as low as zero.
  - ▶ GAE sends to Cloud Logging (p208) a log of the requests made to your app. Since the app runs on Docker and GCE, the activity of the app itself can be logged either by a logging agent (p210) or via the native logging mechanism of your containers. The native option is recommended.

- In both types of the GAE:
  - ▶ You choose only the region where your app runs. Your app is deployed throughout this region.
  - ▶ Only HTTP(S) communication is supported.
  - ▶ You can't use it if your app involves licensed software, since this restricts how you're allowed to scale.
  - ▶ Restrictions on egress traffic are not easy to modify, so you will likely break the PCI DSS rules for companies of SAQ type A-EP and D (p199) regarding authorisation of all outbound traffic. If this applies to you, you need to have "compensating controls" in place to mitigate the risk, or use other GCP services instead.

3.9 Cloud Endpoints

If you design a solution where some info is shared using APIs, you can use **Cloud Endpoints** to apply consistent API management.
- The consistent management layer covers the way API requests are authenticated; the way you monitor API use; and a way to set quotas for your users.
- In a typical GCP style, Cloud Endpoints is actually the name of two alternative services. One service offers API management using the **Extensible Service Proxy** (**ESP**), and the other option is the **Cloud Endpoints Framework** (**CEF**).
- Using **ESP** means that your API requests and responses are mediated via a proxy:
    - It's an open-source proxy, based on NGINX.
    - You can write the API backend code (p8) in any language.
    - You decide where to run the proxy. You can deploy it as a container on Docker (p51), Cloud Run (p65), GKE (p52) or GAE Flex (p44). Or you can get the source code from GitHub to deploy on GCE or elsewhere.
    - It provides API authentication (p5) using JWTs (p9) or Google ID tokens.
    - It also caches requests and responses, and providers Ops Suite services including tracing, logging, monitoring.
    - You can use the **OpenAPI** specification (formerly known as Swagger) to describe your API endpoints (p5) and authentication rules in a JSON or YAML file (the "OpenAPI document"). You can use these to define new client libraries, based on your API.
    - Alternatively, you can specify the API services, backends, endpoints and authentication using Google's gRPC (p27) language and its "proto" ("protocol buffers") format.
    - Note that the gRPC option can run on GCE and GKE, but not on GAE or Cloud Run.
- The Cloud Endpoints alternative to ESP is **CEF**:
    - This framework is for more specific cases, where you work with either Java 8 or Python 2.7, and you want to deploy your API using GAE Standard (p43). CEF is the formal way of creating a managed API solution in GAE Standard.
    - CEF has its own API gateway, which plays a similar role as the proxy in ESP. It lets you define how HTTP requests

and responses find their way between your users and your backend services, including user authentication and monitoring.
- After you deploy your API, you can use the Cloud Endpoints Portal to create a developer portal for monitoring, hosting, tracing and authentication.

3.10 Apigee

I mentioned **Apigee** in the "GCP brands" summary (p30). Two main Apigee products are part of GCP, and there's an overlap between what they do and what Cloud Endpoints does.
- Cloud Endpoints is more of a basic API management service, without bells and whistles, but with good low-latency performance. Apigee offers a wider range of features.
- **Apigee Edge** is a platform for developing and managing APIs with a proxy layer at the front. The proxy handles client requests based on a mapping of your public HTTP endpoints (p5) to your backend (p8) services.
  - ▶ The proxy is responsible for authentication and can also help set quotas and limits; analyse how the API is used; and manage different API versions.
  - ▶ Using Apigee Edge **policies**, you can add functionality to your services without having to change the backend. Policies can do data transformations and filtering, add security, execute conditional logic, or run custom code.
  - ▶ An **API product** is a bundle of API proxies combined with a service plan. You can use the same set of backend services to create different API products at different prices, including free tiers.
  - ▶ You can create API **mashups**, combining data from different sources.
  - ▶ You can deploy Apigee Edge as a SaaS solution (p6) (which they call "public cloud") or in your on-prem data centre ("private cloud") under your own maintenance and management.
- **Apigee Hybrid** is a tool with extended capabilities, to help you manage your APIs across multi-cloud environments, including on-prem.

- It consists of a **management plane**, run by Apigee in the cloud, and a **runtime plane** which you're responsible for.
- The **management plane** includes a UI, to manage your hybrid solution, and an analytics service, to help you understand how your APIs are used.
- You run the **runtime plane** by yourself in Kubernetes containers, either on GKE (p52) or anywhere else, including other clouds or on-prem. This is where you run your backend services, that Apigee call "message processors".
- In the runtime plane you keep an API config "synchroniser" service and a "management API for runtime data" (MART), both of which coordinate things with the management plane. You also keep a database for security keys, cached responses and logs.
- Apigee Hybrid help you use GCP services uniformly across all of these, including access control with Cloud IAM (p178), Cloud Logging (p208) and Monitoring (p211).

3.11 Cloud Pub/Sub

Cloud Pub/Sub is a broker for async (p10) messaging between apps in real time.
- It's typically used for ingestion (p4) of streaming data (p10).
- The incoming data typically describes events (p10) from another system or from multiple systems.
- You use Cloud Pub/Sub as part of a solution architecture which includes at least one **publisher** app and at least one **subscriber** app. A publisher can also be a subscriber.
- Publishers publish messages to a **topic**. They do it because some apps may be subscribed to this topic.
- Messages from publishers enter a **queue** and get delivered to app that subscribed to the topic.
- Messages are removed from the queue when subscribers acknowledge receipt.
- Pub/Sub can manage replication (p7), load balancing (p11), and sharding (p96) of the message queue.
- Delivery to subscribers can be based on either **push** or **pull** subscriptions.

- The pub/sub approach helps create a **decoupled** architecture, because the publishers don't need to know the subscribers. Your lists of publishers, subscribers and topics can change constantly without requiring a change to your solution architecture. The message pattern can be one-to-many ("fan out"), many-to-one ("fan in") or many-to-many.
- Cloud Pub/Sub is a global service which runs in all GCP regions, and can auto-scale (p7) quickly based on message load in each region. The way messages are sent or received doesn't depend on the location of the publisher or subscriber. GCP data centres exchange messages between them.
- Any system that can make HTTPS requests can be a publisher and/or a pull subscriber.
- Any system that can accept POST requests over HTTPS can be a push subscriber.
- Message delivery to every subscriber is guaranteed "at least once", but without guarantee of delivery in the correct order.
- Messages that cannot get delivered within 7 days are deleted. There's no "dead letter queue" feature to send undelivered messages to a different process.
- A message can include up to 100 custom attributes other than the topic. Requests can be up to 10 MB, including all the messages sent in one request. One request can include up to 1000 messages.
- Message pull is async (p10), but a synchronous option is available if the subscriber needs to control the incoming flow. Message push rate is automatically adjusted with a "slow start algorithm", to avoid overwhelming the subscriber.
- Cloud Pub/Sub is often used in solution architectures that also feature Cloud Dataflow (p125) and at least one long-term storage solution (e.g. Cloud Firestore or BigQuery).

3.12 Cloud Tasks

Cloud Tasks is a managed service for distributed (p9), async (p10) computation.
- You use it to define work that can be done outside the main flow in your system. The tasks are actually sent as messages.
- You need to define all the following:
  - ▶ **Tasks**, i.e. the independent pieces of work that need to be done, such as updating a database or running a complex calculation. A task shouldn't be anything that the user sits and waits for while it runs, since there's no guarantee how long it will take.
  - ▶ **Handlers**, i.e. pieces of code to run your tasks. The approach of sending a task to a handler code means that tasks are in fact a type of message.
  - ▶ **Workers**, i.e. services that can process tasks. Workers can be created in GCE, GCF, GKE, Cloud Run, an on-prem server or elsewhere, as long as they can have an endpoint that accepts POST or PUT HTTP requests.
  - ▶ A **queue** where tasks are stored until they are successfully executed. Cloud Tasks creates your queue as an app on GAE (p43). One of the parameters you specify is the region where the app will be stored.
- Cloud Tasks sends to Cloud Monitoring (p211) metrics such as the number of tasks in the queue, the number of task attempts, and the delay in running your tasks.
- You can see Cloud Tasks as the less famous cousin of Cloud Pub/Sub (p47), since they both implement async messaging. There are some important differences, though:
  - ▶ Pub/Sub implements "implicit invocation". Publishers don't know where the messages go and what's done with them.
  - ▶ Cloud Tasks implements "explicit invocation". Publishers decide where exactly their requests go.
  - ▶ Cloud Tasks has explicit message deduplication, retry, scheduling and rate control. Pub/Sub doesn't offer these.
  - ▶ Pub/Sub has an API-based pull and multiple targets per message. Cloud Tasks don't offer these.
  - ▶ Cloud Tasks messages can be larger (100MB vs 10MB).
  - ▶ Cloud Tasks is regional while Pub/Sub is global.

3.13 Cloud TPU

Cloud TPU is a combination of software and hardware that can be powerful for some types of Machine Learning (ML) work (p128).

- The naming can confuse, because Cloud TPU is not a TPU. A TPU (without "cloud") usually refers to the Tensor Processing Unit hardware. This is Google's specialised alternative to a CPU or GPU (p3). TPUs work faster in specific types of math.
- Cloud TPU is the GCP service that can liaise with TPU hardware in a way that maximises its efficiency.
- You should use TPUs if you do ML work that is either dominated by matrix computations or relies on ops that Google's TensorFlow library (p131) optimises.
- There are many scenarios where you should use GPUs and not TPUs. For example, when developing ML models without using TensorFlow, or when using TensorFlow but not matrix computations that TPUs optimise.
- A typical ML model training process (p129) includes many read and write ops, as well as pre-processing and other housekeeping work. Cloud TPU has a "just in time" compiler that improves the efficiency of these ops. TPU hardware will mainly process the parts of your code that calculate loss gradients. Most other parts your code, even if written in TensorFlow, will run on the Cloud TPU host servers.
- Cloud TPU code performs best if the matrices it processes are designed to be easily split into tiles of size 128x128. In some cases, the compiler pads your data with zeros to fit into these optimal dimensions, but this under-utilises the TPU core.

Chapter 4
Container services

4.1 What's a container

At the beginning (if we ignore all those centuries when people didn't use apps), apps ran on servers that used dedicated physical hardware. Changes to the apps typically required some new config of the hardware.

Then came VMs (p6) and servers were "virtualised", so that changes to their behavior require config of software, not hardware. This was an important step forward because it was part of a move towards efficient software-based processes with more automation, version control, rollback to earlier versions if needed, CI/CD (p11), and so on.

The use of containers is the next step in this evolution. It helps introduce more automation and efficiency not only to the way we configure servers, but also to the way we scale them (p6). A container is similar to a VM in the sense that it's a software-defined guest that sits inside a host machine, and still behaves like an independent machine. But containers are more lightweight than VMs, and take fewer resources of the hosting machine. A container can run an isolated app like a VM, while sharing the host operating system, disk and network with other containers. Containerised apps often run micro-services (p4).

The rise of containers has a lot to do with Docker, the popular tool for creating containers. Docker helps you automate the deployment of apps in containers; these containerised apps are versionable, portable and shareable. They are usually designed so that from start up to termination, their lifecycle is part of a managed and automated process. A Docker container comes packaged with everything it needs in order to run your app.

A whole ecosystem of products and services has developed around Docker, and Google's main contribution to this ecosystem is Kubernetes. Kubernetes is the technology that makes it natural for containers to live in a cluster. Each container is just one in a larger fleet of containers that work together, and this fleet can become larger or smaller based on demand. If you're a cluster of containers, then scaling up and down is your idea of having fun.

4.2 Google Kubernetes Engine

You use the Google Kubernetes Engine (GKE) to create a managed cluster of containers using Docker and Kubernetes.

- You can run apps, micro-services or batch (p9) jobs on GKE. We'll call them all "your app" here to save space.
- You use GKE instead of GCE if you want to benefit from the advantages of containers while also having control over the config of your infrastructure. If you want a fully managed service that takes care of all the logistics, you use services like GAE (p43), GCF (p42) and so on, not GKE.
- A cluster may include one or more node pools. All nodes in a pool have the same config and are use in a similar way.
- Each node pool contains nodes, also called workers. The nodes host your GKE resources. By running multiple nodes you achieve scalability, high availability and fault tolerance.
- Your nodes are created in GCE as VMs, and these VMs are what you pay for. You don't pay directly for using GKE.
- Nodes are created from a node image which you choose. There are several "container-optimised" node image options.
- Each node is of a specific GCE machine type (p33), although each type gives you slightly less than its full CPU and memory. GKE runs on each node the Docker and Kubernetes agents, and some processes of its own.
- GKE handles the interaction with GCE for you. If you look at your GCE resources you'll see your GKE nodes there, but you should avoid changing your GKE resources outside GKE.
- A Kubernetes cluster also has one "master node", that has a different role from the worker nodes, but GKE runs this master for you under the hood.
- On each node you run pods. In Kubernetes, the pod is what you actually deploy. Each pod is one instance of your app.
- Nodes are auto-repairing. If a node is found unhealthy, GKE stops it and restarts. The pods themselves aren't self-healing: when a node restarts, brand new pods are created, and they're not trying to recover the state of old pods.

- A pod contains **containers**. You usually only put one container of your app in each pod, but you sometimes add other containers to do work like as log collection and networking.
- You don't put multiple apps in the same container. By deploying different apps separately you make the most of features like auto-repairing, scaling and logging.
- Each container in your pods is based on a **container image**. You can store images in the Container Registry (p60). Note the difference between container images and node images.
- The hierarchy of GKE resources is therefore: **cluster > node pool > node > pod > container**.
- In addition to this hierarchy of GKE resources, you typically also create **services**. Services point to pods, and it's the pods that do the actual work, but your users or other apps will contact the IP address of the service rather than the pod. Defining services separately adds flexibility when making architectural changes.
- You can add further sophistication to the structure of your cluster using **namespaces**:
  - ▶ This is needed if you're a multi-tenancy SaaS provider (p8), allowing multiple customers to use the same cluster.
  - ▶ Namespaces create virtual separation between resources (such as services or pods) in one physical cluster.
  - ▶ You can place the resources of each tenant in a separate namespace, use policies to enforce tenant isolation, and define separate quotas for each namespace.
- The design of your GKE cluster for high availability can follow one of the following geographic patterns –
  - ▶ Single-zone cluster. All nodes are run and managed within a single zone.
  - ▶ Multi-zonal cluster. Nodes run in different zones across one region, but are managed from just one zone. A fault in that zone will not stop the cluster from running, but will delay config work.
  - ▶ Regional cluster. Nodes run in different zones across one region, and the management function too is replicated across zones. This option costs more.
- Your GKE resources can auto-scale in several different ways:
  - ▶ The **cluster auto-scaler** can add and remove nodes in a given node pool. It does it based on variations in the number of pod resource requests (not actual usage).

- ▶ The **horizontal pod auto-scaler** (HPA) adds/removes pods based on metrics such as CPU utilisation or your custom metrics.
- ▶ There's also a **vertical pod auto-scaler** (VPA), which is part of GKE Advanced (p63).
- ▶ **Node auto-provisioning** is another optional advanced feature, that can create or delete node pools.
- These auto-scalers are separate from the auto-scaling of GCE MIGs (p36). It's better to disable GCE MIGs for GKE clusters.
- The key role of auto-scaling highlights the fact that GKE follows a different mindset from GCE –
  - ▶ Auto-scaling, load balancing and other processes mean that you shouldn't rely on continuous work delivered by the same resource over time.
  - ▶ You can design your GKE app for long-term use, but think of individual pods and containers as ephemeral (p10).
  - ▶ For this reason, the happiest containers are stateless. Info you'll need later should be stored outside the pod.
  - ▶ You follow this mindset also in the design of the container itself. You don't install software updates on a running container; you create a newer version of your image or config, and use them to run new pods.

4.3 GKE storage types and workload types

To store data, your GKE pods can use **persistent volumes**. I will call them **PVs** here.

- PVs are the way Kubernetes represents disks. You use them to store data outside your pods.
- PVs usually use persistent disks (p70), but you let GKE manage them and their lifecycle for you.
- The disks can be zonal or regional, HDD or SSD.
- You create a **PV claim** to request a PV of a specific size, access mode and storage class. Then you use the claim, rather than the PV directly, when reading or writing data.
- There are different **access modes** that affect the way your PV is mounted to the relevant nodes –
  - ▶ "Read write once" - a single node can both read and write.

- ▶ "Read only many" – multiple nodes can read, but nobody can write.
- ▶ "Read write many" – multiple nodes can read and write, but the snag is that GCE disks don't support this mode.
- You can also configure PV to use other storage types, and not just persistent disks.
- You can (and should) design your pods to liaise with various databases or GCS buckets (p74), when this matches your business needs.
- There are various GKE node images that support different storage options.

If you design stateless containers, then your GKE workload takes the form of a deployment:

- A deployment is a managed group of identical pods, all running replicas of your app.
- Deployments are for stateless apps, where the different pods rely on shared storage and use the same PV claims.
- Deployments are based on a pod template. The template is based on a pod specification, which describes which files should run in the containers, which volumes the pods should mount, how they should be labelled, and other things.
- The deployment, not the template, determines the number of replicated pods. It ensures that this number of pods are running and healthy. So it's better to use a deployment rather than a "bare pod", even if you only want one.

The alternative to a deployment is a stateful set:

- You use stateful sets for stateful apps, where each pod replica needs its own volume to store the state of things.
- In a stateful app, each node writes data to its own persistent disk using "read write once" PVs.
- Similar to deployments, a stateful set uses a pod template which contains a pod specification.
- Unlike deployments, each pod in a stateful set has an identity that sticks with it. There's no load balancing across the set, because each pod has its own state so they're not all identical.
- PVs and PV claims are not deleted when a stateful set is deleted.

There are other types of GKE workload, alternatives to deployments and stateful sets:

- A **job** creates pods and ensures they terminate successfully on their own.
- A **daemon set** creates pods and attaches them to nodes in a node pool, so that they can run some background work such as log collection. The lifetime of these daemon pods is tied to the lifetime of the node they're attached to.

Here's a bit more Kubernetes terminology for you:
- Most Kubernetes resources are referred to as **objects**.
- To specify an object, you write a **manifest**. A config file (in YAML or JSON format) can include several manifests. Every manifest defines the "kind" of object (e.g. a pod or deployment) and its various parameters.
- When specifying objects in your manifests, you attach **labels** to them. Kubernetes labels have similarities to GCP labels, explained earlier in table 4. They can define metadata such as the release, env, product or your custom metadata.
- You use **selectors** to group objects based on their labels. For example, you use selectors to define which pods will run a specific service (p53). You can define quite complex conditions to decide what gets selected.

4.4 GKE networking

Networking for GKE uses many of the features of Virtual Private Cloud (VPC) networks, which I'll introduce more formally later (p144). This section highlights aspects which are specific to GKE. Amongst the different GCP services, GKE always likes being a bit different.

The various resources in your GKE cluster need networking arrangements in order to communicate with each other. Similar to the wider GCP, we're talking here about virtual networking, which is actually implemented by software and not classical networking hardware. GKE uses different types of networking:
- **Communication inside a pod**. Containers in the same pod can communicate with each other like processes inside the same machine, not using IPs (p8). The containers share the IP address of the pod they're in. They just need to coordinate the use of port numbers (p8) between them.

- **Communication inside the cluster**, involving nodes, pods and services. This is based on internal IPs. The nodes could use the addresses of the GCE instances they are made of, but there are dilemmas involved in how to allocate addresses to pods and services. The result is that there are alternative approaches, further explained below.

- **Communication with the world outside the cluster**. The work of pods and containers is typically exposed to external users in the form of a service. Here, too, there are some tradeoffs, and I explain below the different ways you can give users access to a service.

For communication inside the cluster, GKE takes care of giving unique internal IPs to pods and services. The question is whether these addresses should be ephemeral or dedicated:

- Ideally, you should have a dedicated range of "alias IPs", i.e. IPs which aren't used by your nodes. You can then use this to gives pods and services their dedicated addresses, for use within the cluster.
- Cluster where you direct traffic using alias IPs are called **VPC-native GKE clusters**.
- The advantage of having dedicated addresses for pods and services is that you can use them for firewall rules (p149), network peering (p151), BGP routing (p168) and various security checks without a NAT gateway (p167).
- The alternative is when you run traffic inside the cluster using general routing capabilities (p147), not anything unique to GKE. Such clusters are called **route-based clusters**.
- In a router-based cluster you are a bit more constrained in defining networking restrictions, and if your cluster is large then you might require a large number of routes.
- In both types of clusters you can use **network policies** to restrict communication between pods. These policies are similar to VPC firewall rules (p149). Policy rules can use namespaces, labels and address ranges to define restrictions.

There are two main ways to make a GKE service available to users in the same network:

- Within the same cluster, you can give the service its own dedicated internal IP address (called **Cluster IP**), which other pods can use.
- Within the same VPC network (p144), you can introduce **container-native load balancing** with network endpoint

groups (NEGs) (p158). Requests to your service will be distributed between the pods you include in the NEG.

There are several ways to make a GKE service available externally, to users not in the same network:
- A simple approach would be to configure all VMs in the cluster to link your service to a specific port number ("node port").
- Alternatively, you can add any external load balancer (p156) as a proxy to your service. This approach adds not just external access but also the load balancing capability.
- The most sophisticated approach would be to use the Kubernetes **Ingress** object. In addition to allowing external access and HTTP(S) load balancing, Ingress provides **name-based virtual hosting**, which means you can use one IP address and one Ingress config to serve multiple GKE services.
- If you use Ingress, you create a set of matching rules that define which **backend** handles different incoming requests. Each backend is a combination of a service and port name.
- You can combine Ingress with container-native load balancing. Ingress handles requests from external sources, which are then distributed across a NEG.

When working with GKE, access control to your resources is managed by a combination of several frameworks:
- You use GCP's Cloud IAM (p178) to manage your users and to authenticate their requests, without getting into the detail of the exact changes they want to make to Kubernetes objects.
- You use the Kubernetes role-based access control (RBAC) for managing more granular permissions, related to native Kubernetes types of resources.
- A new GKE feature (currently in Beta), **workload identity**, is the recommended way to manage how your GKE cluster gets access to other GCP resources. It creates a relationship between a Google service account (GSA) (p181) and your Kubernetes service account (KSA), so that this relationship can be defined, audited and version-controlled. Different GKE clusters can have the same Google identity ("cross-cluster identity") or different identities.

4.5 Interacting with GKE

As shown earlier in section 2.3 and table 5, you can interact with GCP resources using APIs, CLIs or a browser console. All this applies to GKE, but you should be particularly aware of the Kubernetes kubectl CLI, which for many users is the main way of talking to GKE.

Architects are not expected to memorise CLI commands, but the dual relationship between kubectl and gcloud (p29) is important. The cluster that hosts your GKE resources is usually provisioned using gcloud, while the detailed config of Kubernetes objects is done with kubectl. There are things you can do with both.

Here are some examples of how to chat to kubectl:

- *gcloud container clusters create my-cluster* (to create a GKE cluster)
- *gcloud container clusters get-credentials my-cluster* (to add a config in your env so that you can start working with kubectl)
- *gcloud components install kubectl* (to install kubectl)
- *kubectl get --all-namespaces pods* (to list pods)
- *kubectl create deployment hello-mate --image=gcr.io/google-samples/hello-app:1.0* (to create a deployment)

4.6 GKE operations

There are different ways you can monitor your GKE resources:
- You can use the **GKE Cloud Monitoring** service, which is automatically built into your GKE cluster.
  - ▶ It includes a monitoring dashboard showing cluster metrics such as CPU utilisation, memory utilisation and the number of open incidents.
  - ▶ It allows you to inspect your GKE resources.
  - ▶ The same service also has a logging option. It uses Fluentd to collect info about your pods and containers and sends it to Cloud Logging (p208), where you can use features like searching through your logs.
- You can use **Legacy Cloud Monitoring** instead, either for monitoring without logging or for both.

- If you use GKE Cloud Monitoring, you can replace Fluentd logging with a logging sidecar. The sidecar is a small container that runs in the same pod as your app and hosts a logging agent. There are sidecar-based alternatives for monitoring too. This is not the native logging mechanism, so you need to manage your logs by yourself, but the removal of the logging process from your main container has advantages we discuss later (p65).
- You can use third-party monitoring solutions, such as the Prometheus "white-box monitoring" service. "White box" means that metrics are calculated inside your app, unlike most monitoring processes that observe the app from outside.
- You also have the option of disabling any ops service provided by GCP, and perform monitoring and logging using third-party solutions or any other custom way.

Some of the capabilities of your GKE resources, like the ability to run a deployment (p55), rely on health checks. They may come with a default health check which might be sufficient for you, but it's also common to set up your own custom health checks.

- Health checks generally consist of one or more probes. Each probe examines one aspect of a system's health.
- The Kubernetes convention is to define two probes, "liveness" and "readiness". They are different because sometimes a pod is running but not ready to accept requests, for example because it is initialising or because requests return errors.
- To let Kubernetes probe them, your containers should have a matching endpoint for each probe, one for "alive" and one for "ready", which return an "OK" HTTP response when requested.

Container images (p52) are often posted to Docker Hub, or other repositories, from which they are retrieved when creating new apps. GKE has its own private hub, Container Registry, for your container images.

- It supports Docker Image Manifest V2 and OCI image formats.
- You can access Container Registry through HTTPS endpoints (at gcr.io) or the "Docker credential helper" CLI.
- Images are actually stored in a multi-regional GCS bucket (p74). You only pay for the use of GCS.

60

- You can control who has access to your images by setting permissions for the GCS bucket. This integration with Cloud IAM (p178) is an important aspect of using Container Registry.
- You can store multiple versions of the same image. Versioning is a key feature of working with the registry because you may use different versions for different releases of your GKE app.
- Container Registry has hosts in several locations, such as EU or Asia. You push images to a host. Within a GCP project, all registries with the same host name share one storage bucket.
- Google run a special "mirror" registry which is a copy of Docker Hub official repositories. Using this mirror, you can pull Docker Hub images quicker.
- Container Analysis is a feature of Container Registry that performs a vulnerability scan on your images. It also extracts and stores other types of metadata. When you enable the container scanning API, Container Analysis automatically scans every new image.

4.7 Extensions to GKE

Kubernetes and GKE are quite a new concept, but things move on so fast that there already is a difference between "GKE Standard" and some newer, extended capabilities. This section reviews several security enhancements and other new features that can now be used with GKE.

Binary Authorisation is a mechanism for ensuring that only trusted container images are deployed on GKE.
- You can require that images are signed by trusted authorities (attestors) during the development process, and then enforce signature validation (attestation) when deploying your app.
- The process of generating the signature relies on the Container Analysis API in Container Registry.
- You can use Cloud KMS (p188) to manage the signature key.
- You can integrate this validation in your build process, for example with Cloud Build (p204).
- You can include this validation in policies you define at the project and cluster levels. You can create different policies for different environments – for example, less restrictive validation in the test env.

- There is a "breakglass" option which you can use in cases where you need to bypass the authorisation policies.
- Policy violations, failed deployment attempts and breakglass events are included in Audit Logs (p209). You can view them in the Cloud Security Command Centre (p195).
- Binary Authorisation is included in Anthos (p66).

GKE Sandbox gives you confidence that your containers work in isolation.
- This service is based on the gVisor open-source project.
- The sandbox is for SaaS providers (p8) that host the containers of multiple customers in one multi-tenancy cluster. The provider can't trust tenants' code, which might try to exploit the permissions that guests have in the host machine.
- The sandbox protects the host nodes from customers trying to "escape" their pods, make changes to the host, or gain access to other tenants' data.
- The sandbox gives the GKE guest an alternative API to access the operating system. This API is similar to the common Linux, but it has fewer permissions. A "user space kernel" mediates between the guest and host, in such way that the container code doesn't need to know that it doesn't liaise with the real operating system.
- Sandboxing has performance impacts, so you may want to consider using it on more powerful nodes.
- When you enable GKE Sandbox on a node pool (p52), a sandbox is created for each pod. Nodes running sandboxed pods are prevented from accessing other GCP services or cluster metadata. You can still also run "regular" pods.
- You can't use sandboxing in the default node pool. Every cluster needs at least one node pool without sandboxing.
- The sandbox is still in its Beta version, and doesn't work yet with Istio (p65), GPU/TPU accelerators and various other features. Some of these restrictions may change over time.

GKE Advanced is a version of GKE with an enhanced SLA (p20).

- It guarantees 99.95% availability for regional clusters. The standard GKE SLA is less explicit about this.
- It includes a **vertical pod auto-scaler** (**VPA**), that can recreate pods with a different CPU or memory to optimise your workload. It can work with or without the HPA (p54), but you shouldn't let both HPA and VPA respond to the same metric.
- GKE Advanced also includes node auto-provisioning (p54) to auto-scale node pools.
- It gives you access to GKE Sandbox (p62), Binary Authorisation (p61) and Cloud Run (p65).

Shielded GKE Nodes go through verification of their identity and integrity before each use.

- If you enable Shielded Nodes in a GKE cluster, all nodes in the cluster have to be shielded. GKE creates these shielded nodes on GCE Shielded VMs (p194).
- What actually gets monitored is that the version of the operating system comes from a reliable source and that the node boot process only runs the expected sequence of steps. A set of **measured boot** metrics describe a known good boot sequence, and the integrity check compares them to metrics from your most recent boot.
- This service is in its Beta version. There's no direct charge for the use of shielded nodes, but these nodes generate additional logs so they increase your Ops Suite costs.

GKE On-Prem lets you run GKE in your own data centre.

- Why would you want to run a GCP service on-prem? Because it adds flexibility to your migration plans. If the same containers can run on-prem and in the cloud, you can migrate on-prem systems to the cloud more easily and gradually, rather than in one big step.
- GKE On-Prem is a core component of Anthos (p66).
- GKE On-Prem runs in your data centre on vSphere, which is a server virtualisation software from VMware. You'll need ESXI and vCenter licenses from VMware.
- You'll also need to implement other third-party tools to address various needs, including –

- ▶ Automating on-prem admin processes (Google recommend Terraform)
- ▶ Applying on-prem network load balancing (Google recommend F5 BIG-IP)
- ▶ Implementing access control (e.g. with OpenID Connect or Microsoft ADFS).

■ Depending on the amount of automation you introduce, you may also need to allocate static IPs for your nodes without using DHCPs server that usually do such things.

4.8 Serverless containers

Some people say that serverless containers are the next big thing. Most people prefer to talk about sports or food, so they don't comment on this topic specifically, but I'll tell you about it anyway.

If you build a container to run an app or a service, the container itself shouldn't mind if it's serverless. The fact that it's a container already suggests that it's a portable solution, which separates the question of what your apps does (inside the container) from where it runs (outside the container), even if it wasn't serverless.

Combining the idea of containerisation with the idea of going serverless means that you can bring along your container and run it on a cluster that you know little about. The cluster should auto-scale fast based on the volume of requests, and you should pay based on this volume, including the luxury of paying nothing when the app is not used.

Knative is a set of tools to build and run serverless apps on Kubernetes.
- ■ The serverless apps you build can run on-prem or in any cloud, with or without Cloud Run.
- ■ Knative has its own build tools to plug into your CI/CD (p11) stack. Knative doesn't dictate what process you should follow to develop, test and deploy your containers – it just recognises container images as the unit you develop and deploy.

- It offers reusable features for *serving* your containers, such as auto-scaling, scale-to-zero and mesh integration.
- It also offers built-in features to support event-based services (p10), with native event production and subscription. Such services are natural to integrate with Cloud Pub/Sub (p47).

Cloud Run is a fully-managed version of Knative. It is a platform for running serverless containers on GCP, on sandboxed infrastructure which you do not manage.

Cloud Run for Anthos (previously called Cloud Run on GKE) is a semi-managed version of Knative. This version runs your serverless apps in a cluster that you create by yourself. The cluster can be in GCP, on-prem or multi-cloud. With this version of Cloud Run you can use custom machine types and do some network config.

4.9 Service mesh

A service mesh is a network of micro-services (p4) that together make up a complete app, with extensive interaction between these services. Many different aspects of containerisation, which we covered in this chapter, can come together when building a service mesh.

Service meshes use sidecar proxies to perform networking, security, reliability and other functions. The sidecars sit in a different container, separating these functions from the main containers of your app. This way, when you develop your containers, you don't need to think about functions and capabilities that have been developed many times before.

Istio is Google's open-source service mesh.
- You attach a standard "service proxy" to your container. Google recommend the open-source Envoy proxy. It takes care of access control, encryption, logging, monitoring, and other operational concerns.
- Istio Mixer is the component responsible for policy controls. You set up policies to enforce rate limiting, whitelisting, blacklisting and redirecting. Mixer also collects telemetry data about the requests and responses your mesh handles.

- Istio **Pilot** is the component responsible for networking, load balancing and routing between services.
- Communication between services in Istio supports **mutual authentication** (mTLS) for enhanced security.
- Istio offers built-in processes for the go-live of your app, including phase rollout ("A/B" or "canary").
- Istio is platform independent, and can run in envs spanning cloud and on-prem. It integrates naturally with Kubernetes and its network policies.

Traffic Director is a GCP managed service that combines service mesh networking with additional GCP features. If you create a service mesh, the Traffic Director gives you with a **managed control plane**. This means it handles the networking side with your own mesh (e.g. Istio Pilot) and also allows the global endpoint, health checking and other features that come with the GCP HTTP(S) load balancer (p160).

Anthos is the GCP branding of a set of hybrid cloud tools and technologies.
- The focus of Anthos is on running cloud services in your own data centre, so that you can plan your migration to GCP more carefully, or implement a permanent hybrid solution.
- It was formerly known as the Cloud Services Platform, CSP.
- Google include in the scope of Anthos all the following:
  - ▶ All the technologies and services included in this chapter.
  - ▶ Most of GCP's load balancing services.
  - ▶ Logging, monitoring and alerting.
  - ▶ Many of GCP's networking services, to ensure good connectivity between on-prem resources and GCP.
  - ▶ Services from third-party providers including Cisco, Dell EMC, HPE, VMware and others.
  - ▶ Kubernetes apps from the GCP Marketplace.
  - ▶ Your own Kubernetes apps on AWS and Azure.
- Because of this "everything is Anthos" approach, I see Anthos as a brand and not a specific service. Anthos does, however,

offer an important perspective on GCP. It suggests that using tools like Kubernetes and Knative, and with the help of the managed versions of these tools, you can run hybrid services mixing GCP and on-prem resources in any way you want.

Anthos Service Mesh (**ASM**) is a managed implementation of Istio for use with Anthos.
- It is a service mesh with less reliance on your own config, and more reliance on default settings.
- ASM offers observability of the health and performance of your services. An automated dashboard presents service metrics and logs for your GKE cluster.
- ASM has a built-in certificate authority to facilitate the Istio mutual authentication feature.
- ASM is supported by VPC service controls (p192).

Anthos Config Management is a "config as code" approach to specifying your GKE clusters and Anthos resources.
- You create files called configs. You store them in a Git repository.
- The config files combine Kubernetes manifests (p56) and CLI code.
- They allow you to specify multi-tenant and multi-cluster policies.
- Using "config as code", your infrastructure can be provisioned in a controlled, automated way. Your configs can be backed up, shared, audited and version-controlled.

Migrate for Anthos is a service that offers conversion of a VM into a stateful set (p55) on GKE.
- Currently you can migrate VMs from VMware, GCE, AWS EC2 or Azure.
- You don't need to pre-build container images.
- The source VM disks are transformed into PVs (p54).
- Google say that with "Migrate for Anthos", migration and modernisation of your traditional app are done in the same step, as opposed to the more common two-step approach. This is not accurate since it doesn't modernise your app.

- On GKE, your VMs turn into stateful set pods (p55), so they retain the stateful nature of traditional compute resources. They do not become cloud-native, ephemeral objects.
- The migration process involves creating a GKE cluster first and then migrating the VM into it. Migrations are configured in YAML files where you define the stateful set, PV, PV claims and other parameters.
- GKE creates a new container from your VM using a "wrapper" image, replacing the VM's operating system kernel with one supported by GKE. Then it configures the container's networking and input/output channels to use GKE services.
- After creating the container, "Migrate for Anthos" identifies your source storage and streams the data from it to GCP. Streaming of your storage is done by the Anthos **Container Storage Interface** (**CSI**) driver.

Chapter 5
Storage services

5.1 Traditional storage on GCP

The GCP services covered in this chapter let you store files of any format and structure. Unlike databases, which we'll talk about in chapter 6, these services don't mind if you store tables, text, pictures, movies, files in formats that are only supported by specialised apps, or whatever. You can use these services to replace the disks and other storage solutions you use on-prem.

Data stored in GCP is always encrypted at rest. This means that if an unauthorised person gets access to the device that hosts the data in a Google data centre, they won't be able to understand it. But don't be tempted to think that now your data is safe; the data faces many types of threats and requires different types of protection. Even if we just consider protection at rest, the default GCP encryption is only one of the measures you need. If your GCP project will be accessed by more than one person then you need to give each person permission to only do what they need. We'll say more about access control in chapter 9, but this is a clarification I wanted to make here.

When you store data on-prem, the classical approach is to have a storage disk attached to each machine, which gives it its own storage space (also called volume). On-prem computers have a hard disk drive (HDD), that persists data to a spinning disk. The mechanical process of spinning the disk makes this quite slow. Most computers today also have a solid-state drive (SSD), where data persistence is based on electric charge, so the things that need to move are electrons (or whatever you call these tiny friends), not disks. SSDs are fast but more expensive, and they might lose some data if you wait a long time. Both HDD and SSD are sometimes referred to as block storage because they rely on techniques that split your data into blocks of a fixed size before it's saved on the drive.

The GCP storage services which I call "traditional" use the same techniques, except that your drives are in Google data centres. If you use GCE then most chances are that you'll use standard

persistent disks, but you can get higher IOPS and throughput with **SSD persistent disks**. I'll call both types **PDs** here.

- Standard (HDD) PDs are used as boot disks, secondary (non-boot) storage disks, and also for continuous write processes such as log collection.

- SDD PDs are often used as boot disks due to their low latency.

- PDs can be **zonal** or **regional**. Both types have built-in redundancy, and the data is automatically distributed across several physical disks.

- You can attach a zonal PD to a VM in the same zone in read-and-write mode. You can also attach it to multiple VMs in read-only mode. PDs are not suitable for multiple writers.

- Regional PDs replicate data between two zones in the same region, to achieve high availability and smooth failover in case of a zonal outage. Replication in regional PDs is **synchronous** (p10), so writes take longer than reads.

- Regional PDs can work with regional **MIGs** (p36).

- Only a zonal PD, connected to one VM, can be a boot disk.

- PD performance is predictable. It grows when you add capacity, but only until you reach the limits of the VM's vCPU.

- You can resize a PD to add capacity, up to 64 TB, but not to reduce. You can add further capacity by attaching multiple disks to one VM.

- You pay for the capacity provisioned, not the volume you use.

- When you configure the PD you can decide whether or not it will be automatically deleted if the associated VM is deleted.

The recommended way of backing up your PDs is by creating **snapshots**. A snapshot is a copy of your PD at a specific time.

- You can use a snapshot either for backup or as a template for disks in new VMs.

- Snapshots are automatically compressed, so transferring and storing them is cheaper than creating a **disk image** (p33).

- You need a snapshot (not an image) to create a regional PD.

- The snapshot of a zonal disk is available to transfer to other regions. You pay for the data transfer.
- GCP stores backups in either a region or a multi-region (p15). Choosing a multi-region gives higher availability and may save transfer costs. Choosing one region is faster. You might be restricted to one region for regulatory reasons (p199).
- Snapshots are incremental. They only backup data that changed since the previous snapshot, to save time and cost.
- When a data block hasn't changed, the snapshot includes a reference to a data block in earlier snapshots. If you delete a snapshot that has dependent snapshots, data that is required for restoring other snapshots is moved into the next snapshot.
- You can back up your data with a "snapshot schedule" and include a retention policy, to define how long to keep snapshots for. You can also create a rule to decide what happens to your snapshots if the source disk is deleted.

An alternative to a PD is a local SSD. Unlike a PD, a local SSDs is physically attached to the server that hosts your VM.

- It's an ephemeral disk for temporary use, with no replication.
- It lasts until the VM is stopped, deleted or rebooted.
- Each local SSD is 375 GB. You can mount up to eight of them (3 TB) to one VM.
- Local SSDs can be created only during the instance creation process. They cannot be used as boot devices.
- Performance scales up with capacity until you reach a total Local SSD space of 1.5 TB. Beyond this, throughput and IOPS do not increase.
- Local SSD is not available on shared-core machines (table 6).
- You can start a preemptible VM instance (p38) with a Local SSD and pay preemptible prices for the Local SSD usage.
- You can reserve Local SSD in a specific zone and get a committed use discount (p38).

You can also use an in-memory RAM disk, which isn't really a disk, but can be used as a temporary storage space.

- You can allocate some of your VM's memory to this storage. The benefit is very low latency when reading or writing data.

- The difference to simply storing info in memory is that the RAM disk looks to apps on your VM as if it was a real drive. So you can trick these apps into saving files in the RAM disk while benefiting from the high throughput.
- The RAM disk shares instance memory with any running process or app. All data is erased on system restart.

I mentioned earlier the block storage approach which is used with PDs. A classical alternative is **file storage**, which is the approach where you create a **file server** (or "filer") connecting a storage device to multiple users via a network (as in a **NAS**, network-attached storage). It's an alternative to block storage because it pays less attention to how each file is saved on disk and more attention to making the entire file easy for all users to access. There are common communication protocols, such as **NFS** and **SMB/CIFS**, designed to make such storage systems work.

Cloud Filestore is a semi-managed NAS file system, which you can connect to multiple GCE VMs, GKE containers or other resources in a VPC (p144), using the NFS protocol.

- Similar to PDs, Cloud Filestore allows you to use GCP while storing data in a traditional style.
- Unlike PDs, it allows multiple users to have write permissions.
- You wouldn't design a native cloud solution with Filestore, for example because it doesn't auto-scale. But if you have an on-prem app with a file server that must move to GCP without changes ("lift-and-shift"), Filestore would be a natural component of such tactical solution.
- You create your Filestore in a specific zone. Any replication in other zones is your own responsibility, based on your availability and durability requirements.
- Performance of Filestore is consistent and predictable. Standard and premium tiers are available, with different levels of IOPS and throughput.
- You need to manage your own backups.
- You pay per TB provisioned, not per use.

- Don't mix up Cloud Filestore with Cloud Firestore (p106), a different GCP service that only needs one typo to get wrong.

There are other traditional file server options on GCP:

- NetApp Cloud Volumes and Elastifile are third-party managed cloud NAS solutions with built-in GCP integration.
- Panzura, Quobyte and Avere vFXT are third-party NAS solutions supported with support for running on GCP.
- You can install any other file server on a VM in GCE, creating a file system which you can mount to other VMs by yourself, using NFS or SMB/CIFS.

5.2 Google Cloud Storage

Google Cloud Storage (GCS) is a fundamental part of GCP. Unlike the traditional block storage and file storage approaches mentioned earlier, GCS is an object storage service, similar to the AWS S3 and Glacier services. Some of the service characteristics I'll list here are features of the object storage concept, not specific features of GCS.

- You can store on GCS files of any type and size. The fact that they're called objects means that a lot of metadata can be attached to files to help use them effectively. The metadata describes things we'll discuss in a minute, such as storage class or permissions.
- GCS is flexible and scalable. Data is not attached to specific VMs or networks. You can give read or write permissions to many users in many locations. You don't need to buy storage space in advance; your space adjusts itself to what you store.
- Typical uses of GCS:
  - ▶ For storing user-generated content like photos and videos.
  - ▶ For data that needs to be accessed by different apps or by users in different zones.
  - ▶ For data that needs to be available from outside GCP.
  - ▶ When you need to store large amounts of data at the lowest possible cost.
  - ▶ When you want to pay less for files used infrequently.

- ▶ When you want each object to have its own "clock", calculating when it needs to be archived or removed.
- ▶ When you want the arrival of a new object to trigger other actions.

- In every GCP project, you can create GCS **buckets** and store objects in them. Everything in GCS goes into buckets. You can create one bucket or more, similar to file folders, but buckets aren't hierarchical. You can't put buckets inside buckets.
- Bucket names have to be globally unique – not just across your GCP resources, but across all GCP users.
- GCS doesn't have a structure inside each bucket, and it doesn't put files in sub-folders like a real file system. But you can add "/" inside file names as if they were in a folder, for example "//my-bucket/musicals/matilda". The GCP console and gsutil tool (p79) are happy to play this game with you, and they'll list your files as if the "/" really creates a folder.
- Latency depends on the distance between the bucket and the user, but it's generally higher than with persistent disks. GCS is not for performance-sensitive scenarios.
- For each object you put on GCS, you choose a **storage class**:
    - ▶ Any object can be in the **standard** class.
    - ▶ Objects stored for 30+ days can be in the **nearline** class.
    - ▶ Objects stored for 90+ days can be in the **coldline** class.
    - ▶ Objects stored for over a year can be in the **archive** class.
- Your GCS bill is based on the number of **operations** (like read or write) plus the number of "GB months" of storage, broken down by storage class. With the non-standard classes there are additional fees for retrieval per GB and for early deletion.
- Data from all classes is accessed in the same way and has the same latency. The difference is in the tradeoff between 3 factors: availability, storage cost, and cost per operation.
- In the "hotter" classes (e.g. standard), availability is higher, storage cost is higher, and the cost per operation is lower.
- In the "colder" classes (e.g. coldline), availability is lower, storage cost is lower, and the cost per operation is higher.

- This means you should use the standard class for data you access regularly. You should use the "colder" classes for data you access less often and for the purpose of backup, archiving and disaster recovery.
- For the exam, Google's guidance is that "nearline" is for data you access once a month or less, and "coldline" is for data you use once a quarter or less. The "archive" class is for data that would otherwise be stored in tape archives.
- In the real world, the tradeoff between storage cost and cost of ops can tip the balance either way. I recommend that you analyse your needs and estimate your expected data volume, type of ops and number of ops. Using these estimates, you can do a quantitative assessment of the cost of using each storage class.
- The operations we're talking about split into 3 groups:
    - ▶ Class A. Ops in this class generally involve setting, inserting, updating, adding and listing things. These are the most expensive.
    - ▶ Class B. Ops in this class involve getting things, reading and notifying. This class is cheaper.
    - ▶ Free class. Ops in this class mainly involve deleting.
- All storage classes include redundancy of your data across different zones, but they vary in terms of the regional spread. Options are to store data in a single region ("regional"), two regions ("dual-regional") or more ("multi-regional").
- The different combinations of storage class and redundancy determine the level of availability (p5) of your data, as summarized in table 7. Durability (p5) is consistently high across all these options.
- I didn't include the "archive" class in the table since it doesn't have a formal SLA (p20) for availability. In practice, the typical monthly availability is the same as shown in the table for "nearline" and "coldline".
- You can create lifecycle rules that move objects to a different storage class when certain conditions are met, for example when the object reaches a certain age.

Table 7: GCS availability and durability

	Multi-reg / dual-reg, standard	Regional, standard	Multi-reg / dual-reg, nearline / coldline	Regional, nearline / coldline
Availability in the SLA	99.95%	99.9%	99.9%	99.0%
Typical monthly availability	Over 99.99%	99.99%	99.95%	99.9%
Annual durability	99.999999999% ("eleven nines")			

- You can give GCS a role in your app workflow by letting object changes generate events (p10) that trigger action elsewhere. You set up **notifications** that are invoked by object creation, update or removal, and these notifications can be sent to GCF (p42) or Cloud Pub/Sub (p47) for further action.

- You can use a GCS bucket to store the contents of static websites, i.e. sites with no compute process at the backend (p8). To do this you need to set up an HTTP(S) load balancer (p160) and map your web URL to the relevant bucket.

- You can enable object **versioning**, so that object updates save a new version instead of overwriting the previous one. But you can't use versioning together with retention policies (p78) for the same bucket.

- Many GCS ops are strongly consistent (p7): you'll never see and older version of an object, or even just metadata, after object creation, update or deletion. If the operation is shown as successful then it was already applied to all replicas.

- Some ops are eventually consistent (p7). These include changes to access permissions and the config changes that result from versioning.

- If you make an object publicly readable, you decide its level of consistency by changing its cache settings. A longer cache lifetime means that a previous version will live longer after the object was changed or deleted. However, note that objects served from a public cache get to users quicker.
- The high scalability of GCS is constrained by some quotas. You'll only hit quotas if you design a very large scale system, but you do need to know the following –
    - ▶ Bucket quotas are stricter than object quotas. If your app generates GCS resources automatically, you should prefer an approach that creates objects in a bucket to one that creates buckets. This also links to the requirement of unique bucket names, which automated bucket creation can't guarantee.
    - ▶ Bucket creation and deletion ops are limited to one operation every 2 seconds per project. Bucket updates – one per second, even if it's just config.
    - ▶ You can have maximum 100 members holding legacy ("primitive") IAM roles (reader/writer/owner) (p179) per bucket and 100 ACL entries (p78) per object.
    - ▶ For buckets with Pub/Sub notifications (p47), maximum 100 total notification configs; maximum 10 per event; with up to 10 attributes per Pub/Sub notification config.
    - ▶ Individual objects size can be up to 5 TB. Uploads to GCS in one request can also be up to 5 TB, but resumable uploads (p81) can go higher.
    - ▶ No limit to write, update and delete ops across multiple objects. Buckets initially support about 1000 writes per second and then scale as needed.
    - ▶ No limit to read ops of an object. Buckets initially support about 5000 reads per second and then scale as needed.

5.3 Securing your GCS objects

There are several mechanisms for controlling access to your GCS buckets and objects:

- You should use Cloud IAM permissions (p178) in most cases where you need to control access to projects, buckets and objects. This is the main access control approach used consistently across GCP. The main exception is when some objects need different permissions from other objects in the same bucket; this isn't the typical use of Cloud IAM permissions because they apply to all objects in a bucket.

- You can create **Access Control Lists** (**ACLs**) for either buckets or objects. Each entry in an ACL gives "reader", "writer" or "owner" permissions to a certain "scope" of users. Use ACLs only when you need fine-grained control over individual objects. A user only needs permission from either Cloud IAM or an ACL to access a bucket or object.

- You can create **signed URLs** for GCS objects using a "Version 4" signature (now in Beta release). Signed URLs give time-limited read or write access to a specific resource. Anyone who has the URL can use it while it's active, without logging in, so this is a way of bypassing IAM and ACLs.

- With **policy documents** you create a specification of what can be uploaded to a bucket. If you allow your users to add files and you store these on GCS, a policy document can restrict the size, type and other attributes of these files.

- If you use Firebase to access GCS (p30, p82), you use **security rules** to specify permissions or restrictions on users' access to resources.

- You can define a **retention policy** for a GCS bucket. Objects in a bucket with such policy can only be deleted or overwritten once their age is greater than the "retention period". The period starts at the file creation time, not at the policy creation time, so older files may be deleted sooner. The retention policy itself can be updated, unless the bucket is locked (see next point).

- You can add a **bucket lock** to make a retention policy permanent. This may help comply with regulatory requirements or prepare for an audit. Locking a retention policy is an irreversible action. A complete approach to object lifecycle management would combine lifecycle rules (p75) with retention policies and locks – for example to archive objects and later delete them once the retention period is over.

- You can place **holds** on objects to prevent them from being deleted or overwritten. You can choose an event-based hold (e.g. to hold an object until a year after an employee has left), a temporary hold (e.g. to hold while an investigation is ongoing), neither or both. If the object is in a bucket that has a retention policy, an event-based hold prevents the object's retention clock from ticking until the hold is removed, while a temporary hold runs in parallel with the retention period.

- A different type of security mechanism is **integrity checking**, which checks whether data has been corrupted during upload or download. This is based on a "checksum" algorithm, which compares the source and destination files at the end of copy ops with gsutil cp and rsync (p80). The process requires a hashing function; CRC32C and MD5 are supported, but only the former works for composite objects used in parallel uploading.

Securing your storage, using any mechanism, requires following the "**least privilege**" principle and other security best practices:

- Avoid giving members more permission that they need.
- Only grant generous permissions (such as the "owner" role in an ACL) when this can be justified.
- Design your solution under the assumptions that any user might try to make improper use of your resources.
- Consider data protection and other regulations that impact your data retention requirements.

5.4 Interacting with GCS

When using persistent disks, local SSDs, in-memory disks and file servers, you access your storage space from the VMs that it is attached to. Once you are connected to your GCE instance, the methods of working with your storage device are similar to those used in an on-prem setting.

To interact with GCS, you can use all the approaches listed in table 5. Of these, it is important to become closely familiar with the **gsutil** command line tool.

The following are some examples for the use of gsutil:

- *gsutil config -r* (to configure authorisation with read-only access)
- *gsutil mb gs://newbucket* (to create a bucket)
- *gsutil cp thefile.txt gs://thebucket/thefolder/* (to upload)
- *gsutil cp gs://thebucket/thefolder/thefile.txt .* (to download)
- *gsutil ls gs://thebucket* (to list objects)
- *gsutil du -h gs://thebucket/thefolder* (to show disk usage)
- *gsutil iam set acl.txt gs://thebucket/thefile.txt* (to define an IAM policy)
- *gsutil acl ch -u AllUsers:R gs://thebucket/theobject* (to change an ACL for a specific object)
- *gsutil acl ch -d viewers-999 gs://thebucket* (to revoke access to a bucket for viewers of project 999)
- *gsutil rm gs://thebucket/theobject* (to delete an object)
- *gsutil rb gs://thebucket* (to delete a bucket)
- *gsutil rsync sourcefolder targetfolder* (to keep folders in sync)
- *gsutil versioning set on gs://thebucket* (to turn versioning on)

you use "gsutil config" to create a config file with access credentials if you use gsutil as a standalone tool. By default it uses OAuth2 (p9).

You can also implement some advanced features with gsutil:

- Breaking down work into multiple processes that run in parallel. When running gsutil cp, mv, acl set and other commands (with the added "-m" flag), **parallel processing** can significantly improve performance if the number of files is large and you use a fast network connection. Behind the scenes, gsutil will use a combination of multi-threading and multi-processing. You can configure the number of threads and processors to optimise it to your infrastructure. In a slow network, parallel processing could lead to poorer performance.

- Performing **parallel composition** when uploading large files. This optional feature splits the file into up to 32 pieces that are uploaded in parallel and then re-composed. Because this feature involves creating and then deleting temporary files, it shouldn't be used with nearline and coldline storage (where the deletion will incur higher costs) or in buckets with a retention policy (where the deletion will violate the policy).

- Creating an **inline pipeline**, so that the output from each step in the pipeline becomes the input into the next step (using the "-I" flag).

- Performing **streaming transfer** (using "-" instead of the source or destination in a cp step in a pipeline).

- Performing **resumable transfers**, for both upload and download. With gsutil this is done automatically for objects larger than 8 MB. If a transfer is interrupted then you can restart it by running the same "cp" command.

- Performing **sliced downloads**, which is more reliable if the downloaded object is large. The standard HTTP Range GET is used.

- Applying a single gsutil operation to **nested subfolders** (with the "-r" flag for "recursive").

- When gsutil sends requests to GCS, it uses **truncated exponential back-off** to manage the retry of failed HTTP requests. Failed requests are sent again while gradually increasing the wait time between retries, until it reaches a certain upper limit. When this maximum is reached, retries continue at fixed intervals. At some point the request might time out. This feature is also used in the GCS console, APIs and some libraries.

- There's no gsutil feature for throttling requests in order to control their flow. However, gsutil allows you do such throttling with the tools that come with your operating system, by setting the maximum level of system resources gsutil can consume. This is worth doing, because features like parallel processing can consume significant network resources.

Unlike gsutil, which is an essential tool for working with GCS, the following are two stepsiblings to GCS.

Cloud Storage FUSE is an open-source project, available on GitHub, which lets you mount GCS buckets as if they were file systems, if you use Linux or macOS.

- Your apps can transfer data to and from GCS using standard file system ops.
- It can run on GCE VMs or on-prem.
- Files are stored on GCS even if this is not visible to the user. This has advantages, such as high scalability, and disadvantages, such as higher latency than local files, and no access to object metadata.
- There's no control of concurrency or object locking: if multiple users write to a file, the last write wins.
- Buckets cannot be used as boot disks.
- Access control is based on auto-discovery: FUSE uses the default credentials found in the environment where it runs.
- Individual read and write ops run approximately as fast as gsutil. By default, files are transferred one at a time, reading or writing the whole file.
- You only pay your GCS bill. FUSE itself doesn't charge for the interface it provides.

Cloud Storage for Firebase is an object storage service offered to Firebase (p30) users.

- It offers typical features of object storage, such as the use of buckets and rich metadata.
- As part of the Firebase brand, features have more focus on the needs of mobile app users, such as resilience to network disconnection.
- Under the hood, the objects are actually stored in GCS.
- Your buckets and objects can be accessed via other GCP services and integrated into the same solutions. Such integration requires access control via Cloud IAM (p178).
- When accessing your buckets and objects as part of a Firebase solution, access control is handled by Firebase Authentication (p186), which is not available via GCS. Firebase authentication has a language of "security rules" to specify permissions.

5.5 Transfer services

There are several services that can transfer data into GCP. It is very common to use GCS buckets for data landing, i.e. to transfer data into GCS first and from there to other GCP data services. But there are also alternatives, such as the BigQuery Data Transfer Service which we'll talk about later (p112).

Transfer Appliance is a physical device for transferring high volumes of data into GCS (p73).

- You can hire the appliance, copy high volumes of data into it, and ship it to a facility where it gets uploaded into GCP.
- This process doesn't involve sending the data over a network (other than the road network!).
- The appliance comes in two versions: 100 TB or 480 TB.
- Google recommend using the appliance for transfer of data above 10 TB. It is for one-off transfers, not for use on a continuous basis.
- The appliance is for one-way use. It can't be used for taking data out of GCP.
- After your data is copied to the appliance, shipped to Google and uploaded, it is stored in GCS in a compressed form, deduplicated and encrypted. To make it useable, you need to "rehydrate" it.
- The **rehydration** process decompresses and decrypts the data. To perform rehydration, you use a Rehydrator instance, which is a virtual appliance that runs on GCE.
- **Data capture jobs** are used for identifying data on your network and streaming it to a Transfer Appliance. You can run multiple capture jobs simultaneously. For best performance, you can run a workstation with a "capture utility" to handle these job. Alternatively, you can export data to the appliance via file systems such as NFS (p72) or HDFS.

The **Storage Transfer Service** is for importing data into GCS from online sources.

- The source can be a GCS bucket in a different GCP project, a bucket in the same project, AWS S3, or any HTTP endpoint that can be reached online.
- The transfer can be part of an automated or scheduled workflow.
- This service is suitable for data volumes above 1 TB.
- It isn't suitable for uploading data from an on-prem source.

Cloud Data Transfer is a GCP offer with a confusing name, which could easily be mixed up with the Storage Transfer Service, but Google use these names differently. Cloud Data Transfer is a general name for the range of data transfer services on GCP. This range includes: transfer using gsutil (p79), drag-and-drop upload to GCS in the GCP console, Transfer Appliance, Storage Transfer Service, various APIs for data ingestions, and the BigQuery Data Transfer Service (p112).

It's important to be aware of the wide range of data transfer scenarios you may need a solution for. The following are some facts that Google use to illustrate this:

- When transferring data physically (e.g. using the Transfer Appliance), speed varies between 1 and 100 Mbps (p4).
- When transferring data online, speed varies between 1 and 100 Gbps (p4).
- With these physical transfer speeds, transferring 1 GB would take between 3 hours and 2 minutes. Transferring 1 TB would take between 120 days and 30 hours.
- With these online transfer speeds, transferring 1 GB would take between 11 seconds and 0.1 seconds. Transferring 1 TB would take between 3 hours and 2 minutes.

5.6 Payment mindsets

This chapter included examples of two different payment mindsets. Some storage services require that you decide in advance what capacity you provision, and you pay for this capacity even if you don't use all of it. Other services only charge you for what you use, measured in terms of data volume or in other ways. Some services bill you for resources of both types.

I'll use this as an opportunity to digress from the subject of this chapter, and summarise how different GCP services (not only for storage) split between these two mindsets. My summary is shown in **table 8**.

In some cases, the difference between the two payment concepts is subtle. My guiding principle when creating this table was to put in the left column ("pay for resources you provision") those GCP services where you need to make bigger decisions in advance. These decisions involve things like creating instances, buying a service plan, or defining rules and policies. In the right column ("pay for resources you use") I listed services where you get charged by the demand for a resource you've already provisioned. This doesn't mean you are charged less, but the charges listed in the right column tend to be more granular and incremental.

Where table 8 lists several bullet points for the same GCP service, you typically have to pay for all these things, adding all costs together.

It's worth noting that most GCP services are charged per unit of time (which could be a month, hour, minute or second). This is the case for most types of resources in both columns of table 8, so I didn't bother repeating this everywhere.

It's also important to note that this table isn't a complete guide on how GCP charge you. It doesn't get into the exact metrics used for billing, or into how the pricing changes based on the features you choose. It also doesn't get into the price itself. These aspects are less important from an architecture perspective. The table focuses only on the two different approaches to paying for cloud resources.

Table 8: paying for what you provision or for what you use

	Resources you provision	**Resources you use**
GCE	■ Per vCPU of running instances ■ Per memory of running instances ■ Per premium image in running instances ■ Note that provisioning can be either manual or auto.	■ By egress traffic volume
GCF		■ Per invocation of your function ■ Per vCPU and memory used after each function invocation ■ By egress traffic volume
GAE standard	■ Per GAE container instance	
GAE Flex	■ Per GCE instance that a GAE Flex app is deployed to	
Cloud Endpoints		■ Per API call
Apigee Edge / Hybrid	■ Based on a service plan you choose in advance	
Cloud Pub/Sub		■ By message volume
Cloud Tasks		■ Per operation

	Resources you provision	Resources you use
GKE	■ Per GKE cluster node i.e. per GCE instance	
Container Registry	■ Per container image, if vulnerability scanning is enabled	■ By storage space used ■ By egress traffic volume
Cloud Run (fully-managed version)		■ Per request ■ Per vCPU and memory used to run your requests ■ By egress traffic volume
Anthos	■ By subscription	
Persistent disk	■ By provisioned space	
Local SSD	■ By provisioned space	
Snapshots & images		■ By storage space used
Cloud Filestore	■ Per Filestore instance	■ By egress traffic volume
GCS		■ Per operation ■ By storage space used ■ By egress traffic volume ■ In non-standard classes, also per volume of data retrieved
Transfer Appliance	■ Per appliance ■ Per VM hosting the Rehydrator app	■ For late delivery of the appliance ■ By storage volume in the staging location

87

	Resources you provision	**Resources you use**
Cloud SQL	- Per database instance - By storage space provisioned - Per SQL Server license, if used	- By used backup space - By egress traffic volume
Cloud Spanner	- Per node in your Spanner instances	- By volume of data stored - By egress traffic volume
Cloud Bigtable	- Per node in your Bigtable instances	- By volume of data stored - By egress traffic volume
Firebase Realtime	- Based on a service plan, unless it's "pay as you go"	- By volumes of data stored and egress traffic, if you use "pay as you go"
Cloud Firestore / Datastore		- Per operation - Per volume of data stored - By egress traffic volume
BigQuery	- Based on your allocated number of query slots, if you use the "flat rate" pricing model	- By volume of data stored - By the volume you read using the storage API - By volume of streaming inserts - By volume of data scanned for queries, if you use the "on demand" pricing model - By the number of IDs imported using the Data Transfer Service from some sources

	Resources you provision	Resources you use
Cloud Memorystore	■ By provisioned capacity	
Cloud Datalab		■ By compute, disk and other GCP resources you use while the service is running
Cloud Dataprep		■ Based on the Dataflow workers needed
Cloud Dataproc	■ Per Dataproc cluster node i.e. per GCE instance	
Cloud Dataflow		■ By vCPU, memory and disk resources used by your Dataflow workers ■ By volume of data shuffled
Cloud Data Fusion	■ Per Cloud Data Fusion instance ■ Per node of the Dataproc cluster used to run your work	
AI Platform		■ By compute resources used for training and prediction
Natural Language		■ By volume of analysis requests
Video Intelligence		■ By feature to analyse per minute of video
Dialogflow		■ Per request ■ By volume of audio data processed

	Resources you provision	Resources you use
Vision API & Product Search		■ By feature to analyse per image
Translation & Text-to-Speech		■ Per input character
Speech-to-Text		■ By volume of audio data processed
Cloud IoT Core		■ By volume of data exchanged with IoT devices
Cloud Talent Solution		■ Per API call
Zync		■ By compute and storage resources used for your rendering work
IPs	■ Per external address	
Cloud DNS	■ Per managed zone	■ Per DNS lookup
Cloud NAT	■ Based on the number of VMs using the NAT gateway	■ By volume of data processed – both ingress and egress
All load balancers	■ Per forwarding rule	■ By volume of ingress data

	Resources you provision	Resources you use
Cloud Interconnect	■ By interconnect circuit capacity ■ By VLAN attachment capacity	■ By egress traffic volume
Cloud VPN	■ Per VPN tunnel	■ By egress traffic volume
Cloud CDN		■ By cache lookup traffic volume ■ In case of "cache hit": by cache egress volume ■ In case of "cache miss": by cache fill and cache-to-cache fill volumes
Network telemetry		■ By volume of VPC flow logs ■ By volume of firewall rule logs ■ By volume of Cloud NAT logs
Cloud DLP		■ By volume of data inspected
Cloud KMS & HSM	■ Per key version created	■ Per operation
Identity Platform		■ Per active user ■ Per phone authentication
Cloud Armor	■ Per security policy ■ Per rule	■ Per incoming request
Event Threat Detection		■ By volume of data analysed

	Resources you provision	**Resources you use**
Ops Suite		- By volume of log data - By volume of monitoring data - By monitoring API call
Cloud Trace		- Per span
Cloud Build		- By build time
Cloud Composer	- Per web service node - Per worker node - Per database node - Per volume of data stored (fixed part)	- Per volume of data stored (variable part) - By egress traffic volume
Cloud Source Repositories		- By user - By volume of data stored - By egress traffic volume
Cloud Data Catalog		- Per volume of data stored - Per API call
Cloud Scheduler	- Per job	
Firebase Test Lab	- Based on a service plan	

Compute   Containers   Storage   Databases
Data services   Networking   Security   Ops

Chapter 6
Databases

6.1 The database language

I dedicate this chapter to GCP services which you can use for storing **structured** data (p95) and **semi-structured** (p96) data, and for processing such data in different ways. Let's start with a few definitions which we'll use throughout this chapter.

- A **database** is a piece of software that lets you organise data, store it on hardware, access it when needed, and apply some processing to it.
  - ▶ I identify seven GCP services as databases, although this definition is not cast in stone. For example, I count BigQuery as a database while Google define it as a **data warehouse**.
  - ▶ Traditionally, a warehouse is defined as a database where you integrate data from multiple sources, and use it for analysis that supports business decisions.
  - ▶ With the range of database features and other data services (p117) available in the cloud, it becomes difficult to follow the traditional definitions. So I don't attach much importance here to where exactly the boundary lies between a database and a data warehouse.
- A **query** is a piece of code you use when working with a database in order to filter data, perform analysis or make calculations.
- **Analytical processing** is when you use a database to gain insight by running queries on a large amount of data. It's also called OLAP (on-line analytical processing). Analytical queries often involve aggregations and joins across data from different sources. They use data gathered over time, to look at stats and trends. Analytical processing only reads data from the database, and doesn't need to write.
- **Transactional processing** is when you make changes to a database by adding, updating or deleting specific records. It's also called OLTP (on-line transaction processing). It involves a large number of ops, each one only covering a small amount

of data. The main emphasis for transactional systems is on fast processing and maintaining data integrity (p5) even when accessed by multiple users. Transactional processing involves both read and write.

- **ACID** is a common set of requirements to ensure a high level of integrity in transactional processing. The challenge with ACID requirements is that they are difficult to meet in a large and complex database. ACID transactions are:
    - ▶ **Atomic** (each database change either entirely succeeds or entirely fails, and there's no such thing as partial success)
    - ▶ **Consistent** (a transaction can't result in conflicting info, even if it affects multiple records)
    - ▶ **Isolated** (transactions can't interrupt each other even if done simultaneously)
    - ▶ **Durable** (changes are permanent and immune to infrastructure faults).
- A **relational** database is made of tables.
    - ▶ The tables in a relational database are made of rows (also called "records") and columns (also called "fields" or "attributes").
    - ▶ The rows have an identifier (ID) which makes each row unique.
    - ▶ Each column is of a specific "type" which defines what values are allowed. Column values aren't unique, but each column has a unique name.
    - ▶ Each table represents one "entity" such as customer or product; the rows represent instances of that entity and the columns describe the attributes of each instance.
    - ▶ **SQL** databases are the most common implementation of the relational concept, so the terms "SQL" and "relational database" are sometimes used with the same meaning.
    - ▶ Relational databases store data in a way that minimises the required disk space, at least in the case where most rows and most columns contain values (i.e. the table is relatively full).
    - ▶ Since relational databases have a strict rows-and-column format with the same columns in every row, they are used

for **structured data** and have a **fixed schema** (also called "schema on write").
▶ Relational databases are not so efficient in the sense that queries often require joining info on multiple entities form multiple tables. For example, producing a summary report of monthly sales requires joining data from the sales table, products table, customers table, orders table, bills table and payments table. So the storage efficiency comes at the expense of processing efficiency.

- **NoSQL** databases don't follow the relational concept. A NoSQL database doesn't necessarily use tables to store data, although for convenience, a NoSQL data structure is still often nicknamed "a table".
  ▶ Instead of rows, some NoSQL tables use **documents**. The documents can also be called "records" like in a relational database.
  ▶ Instead of columns, some NoSQL tables use **key-value pairs**. The "key" is like the column name in a relational database, and it's sometimes still called "column" for convenience. The "value" is like to the value in a specific column in a specific row.
  ▶ A key-value pair in a NoSQL table can be omitted in records where the key doesn't have a value. So if your tables are empty in many places (**sparse**), they may be more efficient to store in a NoSQL database, where missing values don't take any space.
  ▶ Another way of looking at the structure of NoSQL databases is by noting that each record can have different fields. For example, every customer has a work email address, but only some customers have a personal email address stored too, and only very few have a fax number.
  ▶ Some NoSQL databases allow nesting, i.e. storing multiple values as if this set was one value, without creating a separate table for this. For example, if you store a "family member" field for each customer, nesting would allow you to include just one name there for one customer but several family members for another customer, without changing the data structure. It would also allow you to store attributes of these family members. Nested fields can have several levels of depth, so a list of items can count as one item inside another list of items.

- Since NoSQL databases are less strict about having the same structure in different records, the data in these databases is sometimes called **semi-structured data**. The flexible list of fields can be called "schema on read".
- The NoSQL concept was introduced when saving space on disk became a lower priority, because storage became a cheaper resource than computing power. NoSQL databases are designed so that they are efficient to query, even if this requires duplication in storage. You design a NoSQL database by thinking about the queries you'll need it for, and then putting all the data you'll need for these queries in one place. You don't want to join data from multiple tables in a NoSQL database. The semi-structured nature of NoSQL data gives you the flexibility to put all the relevant info together.
- NoSQL databases are built with scalability in mind, making the database easy to distribute across multiple nodes so that they can work together if there is much data to process. Some NoSQL databases are designed as a **column store** (when columns can be stored separately, so that you only read those you need) or **wide column store** (when columns are grouped into families, and some processing is only done inside the family).

■ **Partitioning** a database means dividing it into smaller parts with some degree of independence. Partitioning can be done for various reasons. For example, it can allow parallel processing across the partitions so that query performance improves, and therefore support a higher level of scalability. Each partition may be spread over multiple nodes.
- **Vertical partitioning** splits a table or a dataset into separate partitions, which have the same records but different columns. This way you can avoid loading unnecessary data, and also keep data with stricter access control separate.
- **Sharding** is a common term for **horizontal partitioning**. It divides a table or a dataset into multiple partitions that contain the same columns, but fewer records in each. You'd usually try to partition the dataset so that each shard has a similar amount of work to do, because this

would maximise efficiency overall. For example, if you create 4 shards based on the value of the "month" column, all records where the month is "January to March" will go to the first shard and get processed together.

▶ **Hotspots** are a problem that occurs if your sharding is uneven, so some of your nodes have much more work to do than others, and overall performance is poor. The impact of hotspots is higher when you write data to the shards, because writing takes longer than reading. The risk of hotspotting is high if you partition the data by a column that creates this uneven pattern. For example, if you store time series data, partition it by date and write queries that look for the latest data, then these queries will have to read a lot of data from the same node because your partition key places all recent data together.

■ **CAP** is an acronym for "consistency, availability, partition tolerance".

▶ These are three properties you'd like a database to retain even when the data is distributed and/or replicated across multiple nodes.

▶ The "CAP theorem" says that you can optimise any two of these, but this will come at the expense of the third.

▶ The very confusing thing about CAP is that some terms have different meanings from those used elsewhere.

▶ **Consistency** in CAP is the same as strong consistency (p7). It's not the same as consistency in ACID (p94). The CAP meaning of "consistency" is that you'll always read the latest data, even if it's stored in different places and you haven't checked if one of them was updated later than others. The ACID consistency is different – it's about the impact that one transaction has on different records, for example when moving money from bank account A to bank account B, and it's not about distributed data.

▶ **Availability** in CAP is the same as availability (p5). If availability is 100% then the system always works, so every query to the database returns a response.

▶ **Partition tolerance** is similar to fault tolerance (p7), meaning that a fault or disconnection don't break the system and don't lead to data loss. It's better to avoid this term when possible, because "partition" here means any system failure, and there are better words for this. It has nothing to do with partitioning the database (p96).

- ▶ Traditional relational databases offer consistency and availability, but they don't have built-in redundancy (p7) so they don't offer fault tolerance.
- ▶ Some databases offer consistency and fault tolerance. They replicate the data in multiple places and give you limited access while different replicas are being synchronised, but this reduces availability.
- ▶ Some databases offer availability and fault tolerance. They replicate the data and ensure availability remains high, but this comes at the expense of consistency, because you could be reading data from a replica which is still being synchronised.

- **Indexing** a database means creating a version of it that is suitable for retrieving data quickly.

  - ▶ You don't always have to create indexes; they take additional storage space, increase costs, and can create consistency or performance problems. However, without indexes that match your searches and queries, these searches and queries might be slow because they'll need to scan every record in the database every time you're looking for something.
  - ▶ An index can include some or all of the columns in a table. You decide which columns to include based on what you'll want your queries to retrieve. Index **keys** are columns you can use for searches.

- **Denormalisation** is the practice of saving in the same table all the info you'll want to use when you query the table, without having to join it with other tables. For example, a denormalised table with order data will include details of the products that were purchased, if you want these details to be used in queries. In traditional and relational databases denormalisation is discouraged, because it uses more disk space. In NoSQL databases denormalisation is encouraged, since it simplifies query processing.

6.2 Cloud SQL

Cloud SQL is a managed (p6) relational (p94) database.

- It's the GCP implementation of some common relational databases. You can choose between MySQL, PostgreSQL and SQL Server.
- You typically use Cloud SQL for transactional processing, where ACID compliance is required.
- Your Cloud SQL **instances** can be in a chosen region or in a multi-region, although multi-regional locations are only used for backups.
- By default, Cloud SQL handles replication, failover, high availability and backup automatically. It creates a standby instance with a copy of your primary instance, in a different zone, for use if the primary instance fails.
- You can choose if replication is synchronous or asynchronous (p10). Synchronous replication can slightly reduce availability (p5) but it maximises consistency (p7).
- For your database instances, you choose the number of vCPUs and amount of memory. The maximum you can reach is 64 vCPUs with 416 GiB (nearly 450 GB) of RAM. Storage space can get to 30 TB.
- You can manually scale your Cloud SQL horizontally (p7) by adding a **read replica**. Note that standby instances and read replicas are separate, and you can't use one instance for both purposes.
- You can vertically (p7) scale the storage in your Cloud SQL by enabling "automatic storage increase". It will check your available capacity every 30 seconds, and add more if it falls below a threshold. You can't automatically reduce capacity; increases remain for the life of the instance, so temporary demand spikes can be costly if auto-increase is enabled.
- You can also scale vertically by manually upgrading the machine type, up to the limits mentioned above.
- With "Second Generation" instances, you can choose your zone within the region, and you can choose whether your data

is replicated between zones or not. It was different with "First Generation" instances, but they are now no longer supported.
- Both automated and on-demand backups are available. You can recover data from a chosen point-in-time (but not in PostgreSQL).
- You can connect to a Cloud SQL instance from GAE apps, external apps, GCE and GKE instances, or GCF.
- You can also connect using MySQL clients, the PostgreSQL client-server protocol and standard PostgreSQL connectors.
- Your Cloud SQL instances live in their own VPC (p144). You can give them a private IP address and contact them using Private Services Access (p166) through VPC peering.
- The SLA doesn't cover outage caused by going over capacity.

6.3 Cloud Spanner

Spanner is a different managed (p6) relational (p94) database. It is suitable for very heavy transactional (p93) read/write loads.

- It supports ACID transactions, fixed schemas and SQL queries.
- Spanner's scalability is as high as in a NoSQL database, with automatic sharding and single-digit millisecond latencies.
- All data is stored as complete rows. A "split" is a range of rows that are stored together, ordered by the primary key. A large table might have different splits saved on different servers. With small tables you can define parent-child table hierarchies, so that multiple tables are stored together. You can't directly control the splits but you can define the table hierarchy.
- To use Cloud Spanner, you create a Spanner **instance** in your GCP project. You need to choose a config (which you can't change later) and **node count** (which you can change).
- Spanner is very flexible in terms of its horizontal scalability (p7): one instance can include anything from 3 to thousands of nodes. Scaling is not automated.

- A node is not just one machine: it includes replication across different locations, which is handled by the underlying distributed file system. Replication across nodes is handled automatically. The total number of servers per instance is the number of nodes times the number of replicas.
- Each node provides up to 2 TB of storage. Adding nodes doesn't change the number of replicas but allows higher IOPS.
- From the CAP properties (p97), Spanner has consistency and partition tolerance, at the expense of availability, although availability is still high because of the way data is replicated.
- Your apps can continue writing data to Spanner even if some of the replicas are unavailable. The write operation is considered "committed" once it has been confirmed by a **write quorum**, which is less than all replicas.
- A data manipulation language (**DML**) enables you to update, insert, and delete records. **Partitioned DML** is a specific execution mode that you can use to make transactions in a large Spanner database with less impact on availability.
- Instance config options are regional or multi-region. Both offer auto synchronous (p10) replication, but in different ways.
- In a regional config, all resources are in one region. Latency is lowest if the expected usage is within the region. There are exactly 3 read-write replicas. The write quorum is 2 of the 3.
- A multi-region config reduces read latency if users are in different regions, but possibly at the expense of slower writes.
- A multi-region config uses 5 replicas across 3 regions –
  - ▶ One "default leader region", with 2 read-write replicas.
  - ▶ One other region, also with 2 read-write replicas.
  - ▶ A third region with one "witness replica". A witness replicas doesn't necessarily store a full copy of the data, and doesn't serve read requests.
  - ▶ Any of these 5 replicas are "voting replicas".
  - ▶ The write quorum includes one replica from the leader region and any 2 of the other 4 voting replicas.
  - ▶ The regions must be less than 1000 miles apart, to offer low latency, but over 400 miles, to reduce the risk of simultaneous failure.

- ▶ This setup is fixed. Having more read-write replicas might not reduce latency, since it would require a larger quorum with more traffic between replicas.
- In addition to these 5 voting replicas, a multi-region config can also contain read-only replicas –
  - ▶ You can introduce them in "read-only regions" to serve read requests faster.
  - ▶ They don't vote for committing writes.
  - ▶ Adding read-only replicas adds scalability to your solution.
- Spanner offers two read types. A **strong read** looks at the current version of the data. A **stale read** looks at a time in the past. Strong read requests can go to any replica. Stale read requests go to the closest replica that is caught up to the requested time.
- Availability is 99.999% for a multi-region config and 99.99% for a regional one. The regional config is cheaper.
- Multi-region transactions are guaranteed to run in the same order in every replica. They provide "external consistency", which is at least as consistent as "strong consistency" (p7).

6.4 Cloud Bigtable

Bigtable is a managed (p6) NoSQL (p95) database.

- It stores key-value data in a wide column format (p96). Related columns are grouped into a "column family".
- Bigtable is designed for intense read and write ops. It's not the natural choice to support complex analytics: it doesn't allow joins of multiple tables or transactions involving multiple rows. It works well with denormalised (p98) data: pieces of into that you want to access together should be kept in the same table.
- Bigtable provides low latency and high throughput, so it is useful for storing large logs, transaction history, and time-series data.
- It is highly scalable, and can support billions of rows and thousands of columns.

- Bigtable doesn't support ACID transactions (p94). It provides atomicity (p94) at the row level, but ACID requires more.
- Bigtable is broadly compatible with (but not identical to) the Apache HBase database, and also supports the HBase API.
- You create a Bigtable **instance**, which can contain up to 4 **clusters** in different zones. Replication across clusters is automated and provides high availability. You don't put your tables in specific clusters; they belong to the instance.
- The clusters can be either in the same region or in different regions. Failover (p5) from one cluster to another can be either automatic or manual. You can also route different requests to different clusters, so that low-priority requests don't slow down high-priority ones.
- Each cluster contains **nodes**, all in the same zone. The multiple nodes are for sharding, not replication. Shards are called **tablets**, one tablet per node.
- Nodes are processing units, not storage units. Each node points to tablets on the Google storage system. You can quickly rebalance your cluster by moving a tablet from one node to another, since no physical data copy is needed. You can do this to avoid hotspots (p97) or to recover from failure.
- Each instance is of a specific instance type. The "production" type has at least 3 nodes per cluster. Each instance also has a storage type (SSD or HDD).
- Tables in a Bigtable database only have one index, called the **row key**.
    - ▶ The row key must be unique. Rows are sorted by this key.
    - ▶ No secondary indexes are used.
    - ▶ You retrieve data by specifying the row key or range of row keys, so it's a natural fit for time series data, where you sometimes want to look at a specific period by running a simple query.
    - ▶ Using other columns in queries is much slower. If you need to run queries not based on the row key, you should create separate tables or use Datastore (p106) instead.
    - ▶ The way you define a row key will affect the performance of your database. On one hand, you want related rows to be stored close to each other. On the other hand, you

want to distribute write ops evenly across the cluster, to avoid hotspots (p97). Good luck with that.
- ▶ An example of a common approach is to combine within the row key several fields, choosing a field with diverse values to be a "prefix", followed by other fields you'll want to use in your queries, such as dates. For example, if your row key structure is "username#timestamp", it will have values such as "joharris#20191130", so rows of the same user are likely to go to the same node and form a continuous block of rows on that node, which is good.
- ▶ You shouldn't use a timestamp as the row key or prefix of a composite key, because at the time when rows are written, they all have a similar timestamp, so they will be sent to a single node, which is bad.
- ▶ Bigtable has a "key visualiser" tool that generates a heatmap of read and write ops, shown against time and row key. The visualiser can help you check if patterns of database access are balanced across the rows.

- Columns in the same family are stored, accessed and cached together. So if you need several columns in one query, you should include them in the same family.
- Values in the table can have versions with a timestamp. This versioning feature is for keeping the history of edits and corrections; it's not for storing a time series. Entries that form a series should go to different rows.
- Bigtable is eventually consistent (p7) by default, so a read operation might not get the latest version. You can configure the "app profiles" to the alternative "read-your-writes consistency", so that apps never read older data, or "strong consistency" which ensures all your apps see your data in the same state.
- The storage of your Bigtable data auto-scales automatically, but the processing auto-scales manually, based on the number of nodes you decide. You can introduce your own automation of the number of nodes.

6.5 Firebase Realtime Database

Firebase Realtime is a NoSQL database which you can access directly from client-side code.

- Cases where you'd use this database include gaming, chatting and social media apps, where much of the solution sits on the user's device. Firebase Realtime is for cases where there's no need for server-side processing, but there's still a need to maintain real-time sync between users.
- Your Firebase Realtime database is stored as a single JSON file in a single region.
- It supports transactional operations. You can also use it for some analytics, but as with other NoSQL databases, it's not designed for complex queries which join tables.
- Data transfer between the app and the database isn't based on the common pattern of requests and responses, but on **listeners** and **snapshots**. Listener parameters are defined on the user side. Whenever the database is updated, it scans the list of listeners, and if the data change is relevant to a listener, a snapshot update is sent to relevant users. Listeners are similar to event handlers (p10).
- Apps connect to the database by opening a **WebSocket** connection. The connection stays open until it's dropped from the user side. WebSocket is a communication protocol for two-way data streaming, which is an alternative to the common HTTP (p9). With this protocol, the client only needs to ask once to be informed of any subsequent update.
- You develop the client-side code using SDKs that are available for various programming languages. An important feature of these SDKs is that they can handle loss of internet connection to the client device. They save data on the device and ensure it gets synced with the database once connectivity resumes.
- Firebase Realtime doesn't have a built-in mechanism for replication (p7). You can create multiple instances with your own sharding (p96) process to split the data between them.
- Since there's no auto replication, availability will be affected by any fault on the database side. Consistency (p97) isn't relevant in this case because by default there is only one instance.

105

- The database can serve up to 200,000 simultaneous connections, and up to 100,000 per second. In many practical cases, what risks the scalability of your database isn't this limit to the number of connections, but the reliance on a single database instance.

- The use of Firebase Realtime is charged based on the Firebase pricing tiers, such as "Spark" and "Blaze". Above the limits of the free tier, you pay for every GB stored and every GB of download bandwidth.

- Access control into the database is based on Firebase Authentication (p186) and its "security rules".

- The Firebase Realtime Database is considered an older generation of Cloud Firestore. Although it is still supported, for new apps you are encouraged to use Firestore instead.

6.6 Cloud Firestore

Cloud Firestore is a managed NoSQL database, designed for heavy transactional processing and also various types of queries.

- Firestore has a complex history, which makes its current state quite confusing. You can see it as the next generation of Firebase Realtime (p105), or you can see it as the next generation of **Cloud Datastore** (which I don't cover separately in this book since it's now part of Firestore).

- In practice, Firestore has evolved from both Firebase Realtime and Cloud Datastore. At the moment it can run in two different "modes", the **native mode** and **Datastore mode**.

- The two modes have different APIs, different client libraries, separate indexes, and a separate viewer in the GCP console.

- The SLA and pricing of both modes are becoming similar, and I assume that over time the two will merge into one product.

- Both modes of Firestore support ACID transactions.

- Both modes are auto-scaling with auto replication and auto sharding, to ensure high availability and performance.

- Both modes offer strong consistency (p7).

106

- In Datastore mode -
  - Each table is a "kind".
  - Each record is an "entity".
  - Each column is a "property". One of them is the "key".
  - Access is controlled using Cloud IAM (p178).
- In the native mode –
  - Each table is a "collection".
  - Each record is a "document".
  - Each column is a "field". One of them is a "document ID".
  - Access is controlled using both Cloud IAM and Firestore "security rules".
- The Datastore mode is the most scalable one. It can support millions of write ops per second. The native mode can support millions of concurrent users but has a limit of about 10,000 writes per second.
- The native mode is more suitable for mobile and web apps. It has libraries for additional mobile and web programming platforms. Only the native mode supports features needed for gaming and mobile apps, which I reviewed under Firebase Realtime, such as clients **listening** to a document to get real-time updates, and running uninterrupted in offline conditions.
- You can choose whether your create your Firestore database in a region or a multi-region. Both options keep replicas of your data in different zones. The multi-region option also replicates the data in different regions.
- Like most NoSQL databases, Firestore doesn't let you join data from different tables or run data aggregation queries. However, you can still run a wide range of queries based on indexing (p98).
  - Unlike Bigtable, in Firestore the same database usually has multiple indexes.
  - Every query should be aligned to an index. Running a query without a matching index will return an error.
  - In an index-based query, getting a range of values doesn't require searching every record of the database. This means performance only depends on how much data the query retrieves, not on the size of the database.

- In Datastore mode, "keys-only" queries are efficient in cases where you only need to return the relevant keys, without other properties. In a "projection" query you can get additional properties but still avoid the cost and latency of returning those you don't need. If your data entities have parent-child relationships between them, an "ancestor" query can save resources by only searching the children of a parent you specify.
- Simple indexes, based on a single field each, are created automatically and let you run simple queries. You can also create **composite indexes** for more complex queries.
- There is a risk of hotspotting (p97) when using an index made of monotonously increasing values (like 1, 2, 3 or using the time). More diverse or random values work better as the basis for sharding.

6.7 BigQuery

BigQuery is a serverless (p7) technology for storage and analytical processing of large datasets.

- You can see BigQuery as a modern data warehouse, especially when used with Dataflow (p125) to integrate data from multiple sources and produce analysis and reporting.
- BigQuery has an advantage over the other GCP database services when used for complex queries, that need to process a wide range of records in your stored data. You can perform joins, similar to a relational (p94) database, even though under the hood the BigQuery architecture is different.
- If your analytical needs are limited to just retrieving a narrow range of values, or filter records which can be indexed, Cloud Bigtable or Firestore might offer you lower latency.
- You can modify data (update, insert, delete) using a Data Manipulation Language, **DML**. But you don't typically use BigQuery if you frequently need to update or insert one row at a time like in a transactional database. BigQuery is for cases where you perform bulk updates or you need to process large amounts of data for your analysis.

- You can create tables, views and functions using a Data Definition Language, **DDL**, which is just another name for the standard SQL querying language. The infrastructure behind BigQuery doesn't understand SQL, but an automated procedure converts your query to an efficient series of steps to run on the Google infrastructure.
- Many BigQuery queries, ops and setting changes can be run from the **bq** CLI.
- All table modifications are ACID compliant.
- Similar to traditional SQL, you can create **views**, which are virtual tables defined by a query.
- You organise your BigQuery tables and views inside **datasets**. Datasets are project-specific and location-specific. You create your datasets either in a specific region or in a multi-region. BigQuery automatically handles replication of your data between different zones across your region or multi-region.
- You can create BigQuery batch **jobs** to query, load, export or copy data asynchronously (p10). These jobs run when resources become available. Alternatively, you can run queries interactively at a higher cost.
- BigQuery isn't designed for cases where you continuously change individual records, so it doesn't guarantee strong consistency.
- Similar to relational databases, BigQuery allows you to specify a schema for your tables, and also offers a feature that auto-detects the schema for you. The schema lists the columns in your table, the data type in each column, whether empty values are allowed, and so on.
- Unlike relational databases, BigQuery encourages you to denormalise your tables (p98). You can use nesting and other semi-structured (p96) features like in a NoSQL database.
- BigQuery data is stored in Google data centres in the Capacitor format, which keeps each column in a separate file. This file is compressed, but it can be read without decompression, so searching through large amounts of data can be done faster.
- As we already saw in table 8, when using BigQuery you are billed based on several different metrics –

- ▶ The volume of data you store.
- ▶ The volume of data you read using the storage API.
- ▶ The volume of data you stream (p10) into your dataset. This applies only to streaming insert, and doesn't apply if you load data in other ways.
- ▶ The volume of data that needs to be scanned for your queries.

■ The last of these billed metrics is sometimes overlooked by new BigQuery users. It's easy to make a large number of queries like in a traditional database, and only realise when the bill arrives that large amounts of data have been processed as part of the query. Here are different ways you can reduce this part of your bill; some of these will also improve the performance of your queries.

- ▶ Run full queries only after they are tested using the "query syntax validator".
- ▶ Ditto with the "dry run" CLI flag.
- ▶ Ditto with the "preview" options in the console, API or CLI.
- ▶ Limit your "projection" i.e. the number of columns that are read by your query, by selecting only those you need.
- ▶ Break your queries into stages, writing the results of each stage to a table so that earlier stages don't need to be repeated when later stages change.
- ▶ Perform filtering or joins with large tables first, to reduce the amount of data processed afterwards.
- ▶ Plan your work to maximise use of the cache, since cached queries (typically kept for 24 hours) are served for free.
- ▶ Set up a limit on your queries using the "max bytes billed" setting.
- ▶ Use the free **BigQuery sandbox**, which gives you up to 10 GB of active storage and 1 TB of query processing per month (but with no streaming or DML statements).
- ▶ Define query slots (p111).
- ▶ Create a dashboard for billing data.
- ▶ Monitor usage based on your Audit Logs (p209).

- BigQuery can automatically partition (p96) your tables based on a field you choose – any time or integer column from your table, or the time when the data was partitioned. Then you can use this field in "SELECT … WHERE" OR "SELECT … EXCEPT" queries to minimise the amount of data scanned unnecessarily. Note that "LIMIT" and "WITH" query clauses don't have this effect since they apply after the data is read.
- A BigQuery **slot** is a unit of computational capacity required to execute queries.
  - ▶ BigQuery sees your queries as made of "stages", which are further split into "units of work". It automatically calculates how many slots are needed in each stage.
  - ▶ If a query requests more slots than available, units of work enter a queue and wait for slots to become available.
  - ▶ BigQuery uses "fair scheduling" to allocate resources to queries. Every query has equal access to available slots.
  - ▶ The default pricing model is "on demand" – you pay for the number of slots that your queries take.
  - ▶ You can move to the alternative "flat rate" pricing model, based on a fixed number of slots, if you want a predictable monthly spend.
- BigQuery allows you to directly query external data sources (aka **federated data sources**).
  - ▶ This is suitable for cases where you want to load and clean the data in one step, or cases when the external source is a small table that changes frequently.
  - ▶ Supported federated sources include Cloud Bigtable, GCS and Google Drive.
  - ▶ When querying an external source, many features are disabled, including API retrieval methods, data export, partitioning, clustering, and result caching.
  - ▶ Query performance for external data sources may not be as high as querying data in a native BigQuery table. GCS sources are faster than Google Drive sources.
- BigQuery is suitable for long-term storage of your tables. A table that is not edited for 90 days moves to a cheaper storage tier, with the same cost as GCS "nearline" (p74). You can also specify expiration settings for your datasets and

111

tables. In a partitioned table, each partition is considered separately for long-term storage pricing and for expiration.

- You can export data from BigQuery to GCS, up to 1 GB per file. You can do this manually or with Cloud Dataflow. You don't pay for the export, but you pay for the storage.

- BigQuery comes with several complementary tools, connecting it to other services and providing additional functionality –

  ▶ The **Data Transfer Service** (**DTS**) lets you connect directly to online sources and read data on a scheduled basis. Common sources are Google Ads, Campaign Manager, Google Ad Manager, YouTube, Teradata, AWS S3, Salesforce, Workday, Stripe. DTS supports connectors to over 100 SaaS apps. Transfer from GCS is free. Transfer from other sources has a monthly cost.

  ▶ **BigQuery ML** (machine learning) lets you build and deploy ML models inside BigQuery, using common SQL syntax. A range of ML models for regression and classification (p131) is available. You can directly import deep neural network models from Google's TensorFlow.

  ▶ **BigQuery GIS** (geographic info system) enables analysis of spatial data in BigQuery.

  ▶ There are various third-party tools connecting BigQuery to business intelligence packages such as Tableau. They let you use data stored in BigQuery to directly feed management dashboards and reports outside GCP.

- BigQuery can handle very large datasets, and places no limit on your number of datasets and tables. However, some quotas (p19) might still limit the use of BigQuery in specific cases. The following are some limitations to be aware of, which I've sampled from the full set of BigQuery quotas. All of these indicate the upper limit allowed at the project level (p21).

  ▶ 1000 incoming API requests per minute per user
  ▶ 300 concurrent API requests per user
  ▶ 10 table insert requests per second
  ▶ 1000 ops per table per day (e.g. loads, queries, copies)
  ▶ 1000 DML ops per table per day (e.g. insert, delete)

- ▶ 1 GB streaming inserts per second
- ▶ 1 MB streaming insert row size
- ▶ 10 MB streaming HTTP request size
- ▶ 10K rows per streaming insert request
- ▶ 4 concurrent queries against Cloud Bigtable
- ▶ 100 MB row size
- ▶ 15 TB load job size
- ▶ 10 TB exports per day
- ▶ 4000 partitions per table

6.8 Cloud Memorystore

Cloud Memorystore is a managed in-memory database. It's a GCP implementation of the open-source **Redis**.

- Data is **cached** in memory so that it can be accessed within milliseconds.

- It is a NoSQL database, storing data in as key-value pairs.

- An example of a typical use of Memorystore is for serving live data to game users.

- To connect an app to your Memorystore, you use a **Redis client** in the app code. You can do this in GAE, GCE, GCF or GKE. The client must be on the same network or peered network (p151).

- You can only connect to Memorystore from within the same region.

- Usually, Memorystore isn't used directly for advanced analytics, due to the temporary nature of in-memory storage. But you can produce analytics of the data currently stored, for example the best game result in the last hour. Memorystore can also have a key role in intermediate processing steps of a complex analytical pipeline, managed by Dataflow (p125).

- Memorystore offers either a "basic" or a "standard" service tier.

- The standard tier has built-in replication to another zone (within the region), automated failover, and a 99.9% availability SLA. The basic tier doesn't provide replication.

113

- The replica of your master instance is in a standby state most of the time, to ensure high availability if the master fails. It doesn't serve data to users otherwise. Since you only read from the master, there's no risk of inconsistency.
- Memorystore has built-in integration with Cloud IAM (p178), Audit Logs (p209) and Cloud Monitoring (p211).
- Memorystore currently doesn't support persistence of your data to disk, unlike the open-source Redis.
- Each Memorystore **instance** gives you storage capacity of 300 GB and network throughput of up to 12 Gbps (p4). Google recommend that you start with the lowest possible tier and number of instances, and move to a higher tier with more instances when this proves necessary.
- You are billed per hour per GB of the capacity you provision.

6.9 Choosing your database

As a GCP architect, sooner or later, you'll have to choose between the different GCP database options. You'll definitely be presented with such choices in the certification exam.

Table 9 is a cheat sheet to summarise the different features of the seven database technologies I covered in this chapter. The green smiley faces mean "yes" or "comprehensive". The red sad faces mean "no" or "very limited", and the amber ones are somewhere in the middle. Places where there's no face indicate that the topic is not relevant to the specific database.

In many places, a red face indicates a disadvantage of this option, but not always. For example, some of the options don't support column-based storage, but that's because they follow a different concept, and it's not necessarily a weakness.

Every face shown in table 9 summarises info covered earlier in this chapter. It's important to note that this table isn't a standalone tool, because the topics it covers are complex, and some aspects are too subtle to be simply summarised as red, amber or green. The table may help you remember the details we went through earlier, but it's the details (rather than the funny faces) that really matter.

Some rows of table 9 deal with factual info. For example, there's no room for doubt regarding whether or not a database is NoSQL. But other rows are a matter of professional judgement, and you might have a different opinion from mine on these topics.

In the "analytics" row (*), Spanner and BigQuery are green because they support complex joins and very large datasets. Firebase doesn't support such joins but I still gave it a smiley face because it allows multiple indexes. I've not given Cloud SQL a smiley because it's not a tool for big data analytics.

In the "replication" row (**), green is for databases that offer a hierarchical approach to redundancy, both within regions and across regions. Amber is for databases with just a standby copy for use in case of failure.

The "capacity / quota limits" row (***) reflects my own judgement about whether a complex project, processing very large datasets, is likely to hit capacity or quota constraints.

Table 9: choosing a database

	Cloud SQL	Spanner	Bigtable	Firebase Realtime	Firestore	BigQuery	Memorystore
Relational	🙂	🙂				😐	
NoSQL			🙂	🙂	🙂		🙂
Allows semi-structured data	☹	☹	🙂	🙂	🙂	🙂	🙂
For analytics (*)	😐	😐	😐	☹	🙂	🙂	😐
For transactions	🙂	🙂	😐	🙂	🙂	☹	☹
ACID support	🙂	🙂	☹	☹	🙂	🙂	☹
Replication (**)	🙂	🙂	🙂	☹	🙂	🙂	🙂
Consistency (CAP)	🙂	🙂	😐	☹	🙂	😐	
Availability	🙂	🙂	🙂	😐	🙂	🙂	🙂
Scalability	😐	🙂	🙂	☹	🙂	🙂	🙂
Auto-scaling	😐	☹	😐	☹	🙂	🙂	☹
Column-based	☹	☹	🙂	☹	☹	🙂	☹
Multi-region	😐	🙂	🙂	☹	🙂	🙂	☹
Regional	🙂	🙂	🙂	🙂	🙂	🙂	🙂
Capacity / quota limits (***)	☹	🙂	🙂	😐	🙂	😐	🙂
Denormalisation recommended?	☹	☹	🙂	🙂	🙂	🙂	

116

Chapter 7
Data services

7.1 Interactive data services

We've already had a chapter about the storage options GCP offers you, and another one about the range of GCP databases. Do we really need another review of data services? Yes, we do. Some of the funkiest things that GCP can do with data fall outside the scope of chapters 5 and 6, so I'll cover them here.

It's worth noting that you shouldn't pay too much attention to the way GCP services are split between the chapters of this book. There are many ways of you could group the different GCP products into categories. For example, some people would find it more correct to describe Cloud Pub/Sub (p47) as a data service and not a compute service. Others would say that BigQuery (p108) belongs in this chapter, too, but they would move Cloud Dataproc (p120) somewhere else. The important thing is to understand how each service works, so that you can make wise decisions about whether or not it suits the problems you're working on.

We'll start this chapter with several GCP services that let users work with data interactively.

Cloud Datalab is an interactive notebook, based on the open-source **Jupyter** notebook concept.
- By creating a **notebook** you can put in one place things which would otherwise be kept separately. This includes code (e.g. Python and SQL), outputs, visualisations, comments and guidance.
- You can interactively run code for analysis or for ML model training (p129) in the notebook. Notebooks maintain their state, so the values of variables aren't lost if you perform calculations step by step.
- You can access some GCP services from the notebook, including GCS (p73), BigQuery (p108) and Dataflow (p125).
- Popular data science libraries for Python are built in, including Pandas, numpy, scikit-learn, matplotlib, TensorFlow.

117

- Datalab is packaged as a container and runs in a VM. The notebooks can be stored in the Source Repository (p203), and shared between users using "git push". If you store a notebook in the repository, it is cloned to a persistent disk attached to the VM. This clone the becomes your workspace.
- When you open a notebook, a backend process is launched to manage the variables defined during your session and execute your notebook code.
- When the code accesses GCP services such as BigQuery, it uses a service account (p181) that has been given to the VM.

With **Data Studio** you can build dashboards and reports to visualise data and provide business intelligence (BI).
- You build your visualisations using a drag-and-drop interface, similar to common business intelligence tools such as Tableau.
- Charts in the reports are backed by live data, which can be shared and updated.
- Reports can contain interactive controls, allowing the user to filter the presented data.
- Data sources can include local data files, Google Sheets, Cloud SQL, BigQuery and various other sources.

A related tool is **BI Engine**, which you access via Data Studio.
- It's a UI to manage BigQuery resources and queries. It performs analysis of data stored in BigQuery, and can produce reports and dashboards in the same way as Data Studio.
- The analysis is done in memory, so it can be very fast.
- You are charged based on the BI Engine capacity you purchase for your project. This capacity will determine how much data is kept in memory and available for you to use in BI Engine.
- You can buy this capacity "on demand", including possible use of your BigQuery slots (p111) if you go above capacity, or you can bundle your BI Engine capacity into your monthly "flat rate" BigQuery pricing (p111).

Another related new service is **Connected Sheets**, which you can use from Google's Sheets app.

- You work with this service the way you do with a spreadsheet interface, but have access to the capabilities of BigQuery.
- It works with full BigQuery datasets, which are typically much larger than the amount of data you store in a spreadsheet.
- You use normal spreadsheet formulas, pivot tables and charts to do your analysis.

Another interactive service is **Cloud Dataprep**. It's a toolkit for exploring, cleaning and processing data, all using a UI and without writing code.

- Dataprep is a third-party tool, operated by **Trifacta** but integrated into GCP.
- The data you clean and process can come from your local machine or from GCP sources such as GCS or BigQuery. You can also export the data directly to BigQuery after processing, for further analysis or to train machine learning models.
- Dataprep can handle TBs of data. It uses Dataflow (p125) to auto-scale the resources needed to process your data.
- A **transform** in Dataprep is an action applied to a dataset. You build transformation **recipes** in the "transformer page" which includes the "data grid" (a table with a sample of your data); stats of your data; a toolbar with suggested transforms and filters; "transform preview"; and other tools.
- You organise your work in **flows** that are made of **objects** such as datasets, recipes, outputs and jobs.
- **Wrangle** is a language for data transformation. When you select suggested transforms in the transformer page, they are added as Wrangle commands to your recipe. Wrangle includes various math functions, string functions, joins, unions, lookups, pivots, restructures and more.
- Dataprep has **visual profiling** tools for real-time visualisation of your data and recipe results. These tools help in discovery, cleansing, anomaly detection, identifying distribution and so on. They can visually profile individual columns in a type-specific format (e.g. the postcode format profiled as a map).
- The **predictive transformation** feature shows you different "cards" that visualise what the impact of various transforms

would be. The way you interact with the cards is used to predict your intent and to present improved suggestions.
- The data presented in the UI is a sample of your full dataset. A background Dataflow job generates the initial sample but you can change the sample settings.
- You can schedule jobs to execute a recipe on a recurring basis, and share flow objects with collaborators.

7.2 Hiring a cluster

There were times, not too long ago, when it was common to use the **Hadoop** technology and its ecosystem when you wanted to process a large amount of data on a cluster (p9). There were also times, even more recently, when Hadoop's cousin **Apache Spark** became very popular due to the range of approaches it offered for efficient data processing on a cluster.

Today there are various platforms and products that offer alternatives to Hadoop and Spark, including many of the GCP services covered in this book. But Hadoop and Spark are still around, and there are also products that run Hadoop and Spark clusters as a managed service. GCP has its own version of a managed Hadoop and Spark cluster, called **Cloud Dataproc**.

Dataproc isn't the default choice for processing large datasets even if, as a managed service, it's easier to configure than an on-prem cluster. There are two reasons why it fits specific scenarios, and isn't a general-purpose tool:

- Dataproc handles the cluster config, but you still have a lot of work to do, compared to the way you work directly with BigQuery or Firestore, for example. Dataproc gives you managed infrastructure but you create the **jobs** it runs.
- Dataproc gives you both compute and storage resources. It's usually better if compute and storage can scale separately. There would be cases where Dataproc is cost-effective as a compute solution but expensive as a storage solution.

So if you need either a process that run continuously over a long period, or a job that can be described as a standard query, then you better use a different service. The most natural scenario for Dataproc is if you want to use your own algorithm for a time-limited processing job. Often the purpose of your job would be to run a complex query or train a machine learning model (p129), in either batch or streaming mode. Your Dataproc cluster is ephemeral (p10) and gets terminated, together with its associated storage, once the job is done.

Here are some other things to know about Cloud Dataproc:

- Technologies from the Hadoop ecosystem which you can run on Dataproc include Hive, Pig, Anaconda, Druid, Jupyter, Zeppelin Notebook, Presto and Zookeeper.
- Your cluster can include standard or preemptible GCE instances (p38).
- You are charged per second, based on the number of vCPUs in your cluster.
- By default, data storage is managed by the Hadoop Distributed File System (HDFS). This kind of storage relies on the persistent disks (p70) that are used as boot disks across the cluster. It can also use local SSDs (p71).
- Dataproc also includes built-in connectors to other GCP storage and database services, so that you can read and write data to/from GCS, BigQuery or Bigtable. The GCS connector lets you run Dataproc jobs directly on data stored in GCS. The Bigtable connector has specific links to Hadoop since it supports the Apache HBase API.
- Working with storage outside the cluster (i.e. on GCS, BigQuery or Bigtable) is particularly important if the data itself is needed after the cluster is terminated. It lets you focus the use of the cluster on compute (rather than storage), which is where it is more effective.
- Your Dataproc jobs produce logs and metrics which you can access using Cloud Logging (p208) and Monitoring (p211).
- You can include Dataproc jobs within reusable **workflow templates**. As an example, a typical workflow could create a cluster, run a job and its dependencies in a planned order, and then delete the cluster. The workflow template can include some parameters, so you can introduce some variation between instances based on the same template.

- When creating a cluster, you can set up "scheduled deletion" to ensure it gets deleted after it hasn't been used for a while, or at a specified time.
- If you work in the **high availability mode** (HA), your cluster will have 3 "master instances", so you'll have better fault tolerance (p7). However, note that your Dataproc job is not generally considered "highly available", because individual nodes might have their own responsibilities which aren't covered automatically by another node.
- When you run jobs and workflows on Dataproc, you don't need to predict what cluster size would be ideal for you. You can start with a small cluster and define **auto-scaling policies** to dynamically resize the cluster based on your own rules.
  - ▶ Your auto-scaling policy defines the minimum and maximum number of workers you allow, and your scale-up and scale-down factors which determine how quickly the cluster scales. You should ensure the even at its smallest size the cluster can handle all your data.
  - ▶ The auto-scaling policy also defines a "cooldown period". This period is the frequency in which metrics are checked, to decide whether the cluster should scale. The metrics include the allocated memory, pending memory and available memory. By defining this period, you ensure that scaling isn't over-responsive; you might not want just one minute of high workload to increase your cluster size.
  - ▶ Another parameter in the auto-scaling policy is the "graceful decommission timeout". This is the amount of time you let a job keep running after it's been decided to remove the node it runs on.
  - ▶ You create your auto-scaling policy as a YAML file and implement it with gcloud (p29).
  - ▶ You can apply the same policy to multiple clusters (in the same region). If the clusters share similar workflows then this is the recommended practice.
  - ▶ Auto-scaling works best when your storage is not on the cluster, e.g. in GCS or BigQuery.
  - ▶ Auto-scaling is for use in standard clusters running batch jobs; not in the HA mode or with Spark streaming data.

- ▶ You can (and should) configure auto-scaling to scale your cluster down when the cluster is temporarily idle; but note that scaling down is not for when the job is done. Dataproc clusters are meant to be ephemeral resources, so you should ensure the cluster is removed when it has finished a job, preferably as part of an automated workflow or a using the scheduled deletion feature.
- ■ When you create a Dataproc cluster, you can enable the **Hadoop Secure Mode via Kerberos**.
  - ▶ Kerberos is an authentication protocol developed by Microsoft.
  - ▶ The Dataproc Kerberos mode makes your cluster more suitable for hosting multiple tenants. It implements user authentication (p5) and encryption.
  - ▶ The authentication and the multi-tenancy only apply within the cluster; interaction with other GCP services is authenticated with the identity of the service account (p181) of the cluster.
  - ▶ Enabling Kerberos creates an on-cluster Key Distribution Centre (KDC) with "service principals" (users) and a "root principal" (account admin). You can add these principals manually, or establish a "cross-realm trust" with an external KDC which already has its own principals.
  - ▶ When you enable the Kerberos mode, Dataproc creates a "self-signed" SSL certificate (p9) to enable cluster encryption. You can provide an alternative certificate.
  - ▶ In the HA mode, a Kerberos cluster will have one "master" KDC, which also serves as the admin server, and two "slave" KDCs that get synced with the master. All 3 KDCs will serve read traffic.

7.3 Data pipeline services

You can achieve powerful outcomes by automating processes that involves different data manipulation steps, so that the output from each step is the input into the following step. Such multi-stage processes are sometimes called **data pipelines**.

Traditional, on-prem data pipelines are used to integrate data from multiple sources and store it in a data warehouse. This process is widely known as "extract-transform-load" (**ETL**). The data integrated via ETL is typically used for analytics, business intelligence, and the development of machine learning models.

Data pipelines in the cloud, too, run ETL processes and serve similar purposes. Cloud-based pipelines sometimes combine an even wider range of data sources and processing steps, both on-prem and elsewhere.

In this section I'll cover Apache Beam, Cloud Dataflow and Cloud Data Fusion, all of which let you create pipelines. Note that Cloud Composer (p205) could feel at home here, too, but it also has family in chapter 10, so I'll cover it there. Another pipeline tool, **Kubeflow**, is available via the **AI Hub** (p131).

Apache Beam is a tool for creating data pipelines. The techniques behind it were developed by Google, but it is available as an open-source tool.

- You can use Beam to develop either batch (p9) or streaming (p10) data pipelines.
- Beam is used for defining the pipeline, not for implementing it. A **runner** is the tool that executes a Beam pipeline. You can use services like Dataflow (p125) as the runner of the pipeline.
- You often use Beam for pipelines that run distributed processes on a cluster. Beam can handle for you the coordination of work across the cluster and operations such as partitioning and sharding (p96).
- You define your Bean pipeline in a **driver program**. In the program you create a pipeline **object**. Each pipeline represents a single, repeatable job. Within the pipeline, a **PCollection** represents a dataset.
- A **transform** takes one or more PCollections as input, performs an operation that you specify, and produces one or more PCollections as output. The operation may involve some computation, grouping, reading, writing, filtering and so on.
- An operation in a transform can be a transform in itself, so there can be a hierarchy of transforms in your pipeline, each one starting with a "read" and ending with a "write".

- A **ParDo** is the core processing operation. It applies a user-defined function to each element of the input PCollection, with the option of doing this in parallel.
- In a processing operation you can use **DoFn**. A DoFn is any small function you code, which only depends on its direct inputs and has no side effects other than its direct output.
- **I/O connectors** let you read data into your pipeline and write output data from it. An I/O connector consists of a source and a **sink** (destination), both are types of transforms.
- **Windowing** splits a PCollection into individual elements ("windows"), and is different from partitioning. Windowing is done for transforms (such as "group by" aggregations) that need to do some separate intermediate processing for each window. A windowing function defines how to window and how to merge windows.
- A **watermark** is an event (p10) that means all data in a certain window has entered the pipeline. Beam tracks this so that it can process data consistently even when input data hasn't arrived in an organised way.
- **Triggers** determine when the outputs from a window are ready. By default, results are ready once the full input has been processed, but sometimes the input is "unbounded", i.e. arriving continuously so you never have the full input. In such cases readiness can be assessed, for example, by comparing the timestamp of the watermark to the range of timestamps of data in the window. Beam provides several predefined triggers and also lets you combine them. Triggers are useful in cases where data arrival patterns are unpredictable and include some parts of the data arriving late.

Cloud Dataflow is a GCP service for building and executing data pipelines. You can use Dataflow to process both batch and real-time streaming data. You can connect your pipeline to other GCP services as your data sources and sinks.
- Dataflow is serverless. You don't configure the resources that execute your pipeline, and you only pay for what you use.
- You can use Dataflow to execute pipelines built with Apache Beam. The combination of Beam and Dataflow is a natural choice for pipelines where you want to implement features like

windowing and triggers (p125), e.g. when data arrival patterns might be unpredictable.
- Dataflow runs your pipeline on GCE instances. You can specify the zone and network where your instances are created.
- The code where you've defined your pipeline is converted by Dataflow into an **execution graph**. In this graph, Dataflow may take your transforms (p124) through some "fusions" and "optimisations" before it turns it into a **job**.
- In addition to the optimisation of your pipeline in the execution graph, Dataflow may also perform **dynamic work rebalancing** while the job runs, if the job includes parallel processing. The rebalancing involves moving work from one instance to another based on info collected in real time.
- Different elements of your pipeline may be grouped arbitrarily into **bundles** that are processed together. If a specific element fails, the whole bundle is tried again. In batch mode, bundles get 4 re-try opportunities. In streaming mode, they are re-tried indefinitely (which may actually cause trouble).
- You can enable the Dataflow **Streaming Engine**, which moves the execution of your pipeline from your GCE worker VMs to the Dataflow backend, for an extra cost. When your pipeline runs this way, it uses vCPUs, memory and storage resources more efficiently, and its auto-scaling behaviour is smoother. The Streaming Engine works best in jobs that use small machine types and no persistent disk storage.
- You can enable **auto-scaling** so that your number of workers adjusts itself to the pipeline workload. In batch mode you'll pay for the <u>average</u> number of GCE instances and the <u>maximum</u> number of persistent disks you use. In streaming mode, auto-scaling is free if you use the Streaming Engine.
- The ability of your pipeline to scale up depends on the number of persistent disks you created with the pipeline. There have to be enough disks for all workers also after additional workers have been created.
- "Shuffle" is the operation behind transforms like "group" and "combine". It partitions and groups data by key in an efficient way. The Dataflow batch mode has a service also called **Shuffle**, which moves the shuffle operation from the VMs to a

Dataflow backend for an extra charge. When you use this feature, your VMs can use smaller disks.
- Pipelines can also run on your local machine, for example if you want to test them on a small dataset.
- Dataflow **FlexRS** reduces batch processing costs with the help of advanced scheduling. When you submit a FlexRS job, it is first placed in a queue. The time when it gets executed is based on capacity and cost optimisation. FlexRS jobs also use the Shuffle service and a mix of preemptible and regular VMs.
- **Dataflow SQL** (currently in a Beta pre-release) makes it possible to build pipelines using familiar SQL code, the same as the SQL dialect used in BigQuery. It also automatically detects the need for batch or stream data processing.
- Dataflow uses two service accounts (p181) for access control: the Dataflow service account and the "controller" service account. The Dataflow account creates and changes GCP resources on your behalf. The controller account is used by the GCE instances running the job. You need to ensure that the controller account has access to resources such as GCS buckets, BigQuery datasets and Pub/Sub topics.
- If your pipeline uses resources owned by another GCP project, you should use Cloud IAM to define cross-project permissions.
- All communication with GCP sources and sinks uses HTTPS.
- All communication between workers runs within a private network, and is subject to your project's permissions and firewall rules.
- As a default, GCE instances and disks are deleted when the Dataflow job completes.

Cloud Data Fusion is a different managed service for data integration and for building data pipelines.
- It is based on an open-source project called CDAP.
- A key difference between Dataflow and Data Fusion is that you design your Data Fusion pipelines visually using a graphical UI, unlike the code-based Dataflow.
- A **plugin** is a customisable module that can be used in a pipeline. Plugins can represent data sources, data sinks, data transformations, analytical tasks, conditions, "error collectors", "alert publishers". You can also build custom plugins.

127

- Each action in the pipeline is a **node**. Each node contains a **plugin**. The Data Fusion UI lets you connect nodes to create complete pipelines. It's important to note the consuming terminology: a "node" here is not a cluster node.
- Data Fusion runs on Dataproc (p120). Your pipeline is converted into a graph with parallel computations that can use both batch and real-time capabilities of Dataproc.
- You create Cloud Data Fusion **instances** in the GCP console (p27). Each instance is deployed independently. Behind the scenes, your instances are deployed on GKE (p52).
- It uses GCS, Cloud SQL and persistent disks to store metadata, and also KMS (p188) and Audit Logs (p209).
- Your pipeline gets executed in an ephemeral **execution environment**. These envs are deleted when execution is complete. A "compute profile" specifies your env (cluster, credentials, memory, vCPU, image, node count).
- If you've already created Dataproc clusters, you can use them instead as **controlled envs**.
- There are built-in connectors to various data sources and sinks: GCS, BigQuery, Cloud SQL, Pub/Sub, Spanner, Bigtable, Datastore, as well as non-GCP cloud services, file systems and database technologies.

7.4 Artificial intelligence

When businesses decide to store data and run pipelines on GCP, one of their most common objectives is to use these as the basis for developing **artificial intelligence** (**AI**) using **machine learning** (**ML**).

Before we review GCP services in this area, let's clarify some terminology.
- **AI** is a very broad term. It may describe any system that can automatically perform tasks which require systematic logical reasoning, equivalent to human intelligence or stronger.
  - ▶ Not every automated solution has AI. An AI solution applies a series of intelligent capabilities automatically, in a strategic way.

- ▶ For example: you may develop an AI solution that continuously ingests info, understands what it has read, learns from it, remembers what it learned, plans when to use what it remembers, makes decisions based on the plan, and implements the decisions in a way that meets business objectives.
- ▶ So if an app can read a paragraph you wrote and correct your grammar, I'm not sure it has AI because it might be just blindly applying a set of grammatical correction rules. But if your app reads your paragraph and tells you which famous author your writing style is like, then it's more likely that there's some AI behind it.
- ▶ Similarly, if you want to create an app that gets a video of a football match and creates a shorter version without the boring parts, you may be able to develop it without AI, by automatically analysing how noisy the crowd is. But for an app that creates a shorter video that only includes goal attempts by your favourite player, you probably need AI.

■ **ML** is a subset of the capabilities that can add AI to a solution. ML is all about automatically learning from data so that later you can automatically implement what was learned. ML includes a wide range of techniques for identifying patterns in data you already have, so that later you can apply this learning to new data.

- ▶ Not every data analysis is ML. To develop ML, you need to find sufficient statistical evidence of some consistent trends or behaviours in your data. These learned behaviours may then be applied, under some conditions, to predict what happens in some new situations.
- ▶ I mentioned earlier an app that compares the style of a paragraph to the writing styles of famous authors. To develop it, you'll need to build a ML **model** that can associate a paragraph with an author. You'll need to **train** this model using a dataset containing many paragraphs by many authors. You'll need to **label** each paragraph with the name of the author, so that the model can learn what features of each paragraph can explain who wrote it. If your model training process is successful, your app can then **apply** this model to new paragraphs, trying to **predict** which author may have written them.
- ▶ To develop an app that extracts from a football video only the goals by a specific player, you'll need to build a ML

model that can scan a video, detect sections with goals and also detect and recognise the player making the goal. You'll need to **train** this model using a dataset containing many video sections with and without goals, with different players, with **labels** indicating whether or not each section contains a goal and who the player is. If you've managed to train such model, you can then use it for **prediction** with new inputs that aren't labelled. The model will try to **infer** the missing label.

▶ It's important to note that **labelling** is always a manual process. Your data items need to have labels that indicate what you want your ML model to learn to predict automatically. If you were able to add the labels automatically in the first place, then you already have a ML model, so there wouldn't be a need to add labels now. A powerful way to label is to let your users do it: if a user tagged a photo with their name, and you use user photos to train a model to identify their faces, then they've done the labelling work for you. Or if your model aims to predict which songs a user will like, their "like" history gives you the labels. But if you want to predict something that hasn't already been added to the data by somebody else, you'll need to do it yourself manually.

▶ Model training is computationally much more challenging than applying a model you've already trained. That's because the training process typically needs to read many thousands of labelled inputs, and also run through each of them multiple times, until it is able to find statistically-significant patterns in the data. Application of an existing model doesn't require this search process.

▶ On the other hand, the training process usually doesn't need to be done in real time. You can schedule a batch process to train your model once a day, based on the latest data available when the batch job runs. Prediction is often needed in real time, for example if you want the model to recommend the most suitable products to a customer during their short visit to your website.

▶ A common family of ML models perform **classification** of data items. Classification models learn how the data splits between different categories. This can help, for example,

distinguish between a movie that a user will probably like and a movie they won't; or to suggest whether or not the findings of a medical test show signs of a disease.
  ▶ Another common family of ML models perform **regression**. Regression models predict quantitative values, such as the chance that a certain customer will buy your competitor's products or the expected number of calls to your helpdesk during the weekend.
- Some of the most common AI/ML challenges today involve **computer vision** (to automatically understand photos and videos); **natural language processing** (to understand texts or produce new meaningful texts); and problems of searching for relevant into in large unstructured datasets. GCP offers some specialised services in these areas.
- **Deep learning models** use the mathematical concept of **artificial neural networks** to solve complex classification or regression problems. There are specific types of deep learning models tailored for computer vision and natural language problems.
- **TensorFlow** is a code library for a range of mathematical uses and primarily for training ML models. It's an open-source project created by Google. TensorFlow has a central role as a ML modelling language in GCP, mainly using Python, but is also available on other platforms and other programming languages.

The **AI Hub** on GCP is an access point to various components you can include in a data pipeline with ML capabilities.
- The AI hub is still in its Beta release.
- The pipelines you build are based on **Kubeflow**, an open-source platform that Google developed for building AI systems and deploying them on Kubernetes (p51). The Kubernetes apps you develop are highly portable and scalable.
- Kubeflow and the hub let you include in your ML workflow the AI services that GCP offers, as well as TensorFlow modules.
- As part of your development work, you can create experiments in interactive Jupyter notebooks (p117).
- Your pipeline can cover the whole lifecycle of a ML model, including data preparation, model training, production of model stats and outputs, and prediction using a trained model.

- The hub has sharing features, allowing colleagues to work collaboratively with the same ML pipeline components.
- AI Hub also offers pre-packaged VM images with an AI environment to run your pipelines on. Your VMs can use Cloud TPU (p50) or GPU (p3) to improve performance.
- The AI Hub has some similarities to the TensorFlow Hub, which has its origins in Google but is not part of GCP. However, the AI Hub is a service with wider capabilities, not only those linked to TensorFlow.

The **AI Platform** is a collection of tools for building ML models, hosting them and using them to make predictions.
- It includes the service formerly known as ML Engine.
- You can easily confuse the AI Platform and the AI Hub. The AI Platform supports **Kubeflow** like the AI Hub, but the hub is for organising components to form a pipeline, whereas the platform is where you can create such components.
- The AI Platform offers several services –
  - ▶ Model **training** using either built-in algorithms or your own custom training job, which can run on the platform. The built-in algorithms don't require writing any code, but they are restricted to running on the platform's specific machine types. The models are implemented in TensorFlow. If you create your custom training job, you can use the "distributed training" structure which runs your job on a training cluster, and a "hyperparameter tuning" service to improve the efficiency of the search for optimal model parameters. You can download your models and use them for prediction outside GCP.
  - ▶ Serving **prediction** outputs to your apps based on a trained model, also if the model was developed elsewhere. You can make either batch or real-time online predictions. You create a "model" resource and a "version" resource within it, to serve your predictions. You can monitor predictions on a continuous basis.
  - ▶ Running **notebooks**, where you can combine code, inputs, outputs, analysis and documentation. The platform offers a VM image that comes with built-in notebooks.

- ▶ Training **deep learning** models for you, in a similar way to the training service, but using a VM type that was designed for the complexity of these models.
- ▶ A data **labelling** service, which I wish Google didn't present as part of the AI Platform, because it's all about Google hiring people to do the manual work of adding labels (p130) to your data, if you can't do it by yourself. You need to provide them with instructions on how to label your data and include some examples.
- When AI Platform runs a training job, it logs info about inputs and outputs, and stores it using Cloud Logging (p208). Viewing the log can help you understand the behaviour of your training code. You can also inspect the log using the **TensorBoard** tools that come with TensorFlow.

A range of GCP services specialise in specific areas of AI. These services are named in a way that can confuse, since the name mixes the AI capability (e.g. vision, translation, natural language) with Google's **AutoML** brand for a subset of the services. Here's an overview, followed by more detail on each service:

- The services with AutoML in the name are those that you can customise using your own data. They offer **transfer learning**: your starting point is a model that Google have already trained, but you can do further training with your own data, so that your final model benefits from both Google's global wisdom and your own specific data points.
- **Cloud Vision** includes the Cloud Vision API, AutoML Vision, AutoML Vision Edge, and the Cloud Vision API Product Search.
- **Cloud Translation** includes the Basic Translation API, Advanced Translation API and AutoML Translation.
- **Natural Language** (sometimes without "Cloud"!) includes the Natural Language API and AutoML Natural Language.
- **Cloud Video Intelligence** includes the Video Intelligence API and AutoML Video Intelligence.
- Another AutoML service is AutoML Tables.
- There are several other GCP services related to natural language processing: Dialogflow, Cloud Speech-to-Text and Cloud Text-to-Speech. They aren't part of AutoML, and Google also don't list them under the Natural Language service, but they are strongly related all the same.

- All of these evolve quickly, and I wouldn't be surprised if by the time you read this, the GCP AI services will have been renamed again!
- All of these are managed services, and they are mainly for users who are not ML experts or data scientists. Even when you use AutoML to customise your model, you still have limited ability to view the model parameters you estimate in the training process, and you can only see a high-level summary of the statistical performance of your model.
- ML experts will typically create their own Python code for model training, so that they can look at their model from the inside. These advanced users will still benefit from some of the advanced features of the AI Hub and AI Platform, such as distributed training.
- When deploying your model and serving predictions to your apps, the difference between a ML expert and a user that relies on Google's pre-trained models is smaller. Many types of users can benefit from deploying their model (whichever way it was trained) as a managed service. They can then embed API calls to this service in the apps they develop, either on GCP (for example using GAE or GKE) or elsewhere.

The **Cloud Vision API** gives you access to a trained ML model that estimates what's shown in images you provide.
- It can classify your images based on a large group of categories that have been defined by Google.
- The API can detect objects, indicate where in the photo the object is, identify famous places, identify common logos, detect faces in the photo (without knowing who they are), and suggest who they are if they are public figures.
- It can read text that appears in a photo using an Optical Character Recognition (OCR) technique.
- It can return multiple results per image, if it shows multiple items or if there is doubt about what these items might be.
- If you need to customise the model, use AutoML instead.

AutoML Vision lets you train ML models to classify images according to your own defined labels. You can register your trained models for serving through the AutoML API.

AutoML Vision Edge is for use in cases where you need to deploy your vision model on an **edge device**.
- An edge device is a machine with limited compute power, memory or connectivity, such as a sensor used in a car.
- AutoML Vision Edge optimises the deployed model so that its resource requirements are minimal.
- You can also use it when building Firebase (p30) apps for iOS or Android devices, as part of the **Firebase ML Kit**.

Cloud Vision Product Search is for use in retail apps. It lets customers search for a product similar to an image they provide.
- The retailer creates **products** with **reference images**, visually describing the product from a set of viewpoints.
- The retailer can add these products to **product sets**, so that each product set can be searched separately.
- When users run a query with their own image, Cloud Vision Product Search uses ML to compare the user's image with the images in the product set. It returns a ranked list of similar results. Similarity can be either visual or semantic.
- A version of this service is available for mobile front-end users via the Firebase ML Kit.

The **Basic Translation API** lets you use the Google Translate ML service in your own app or website.
- It supports over 100 languages.
- Using it is subject to a strict set of attribution and disclaimer requirements.

The **Advanced Translation API** includes the features of the basic one, but it also supports some customisation features. You can provide your own glossary, with terms used in your field or domain, and they become available for use in translation.

AutoML Translation is for use when you want to create your own custom translation model. Based on matching pairs of words or sentences you provide in the source and target languages, a new translation model is trained for you.

The **Natural Language API** gives you access to pre-trained models that can analyse and annotate a text you provide.
- It can perform syntax analysis, entity analysis, sentiment analysis and content classification of your text.
- About 10 languages were supported last time I checked.
- **Syntax analysis** splits the text into basic units known as tokens (typically one word per token), and returns for each token the part-of-speech; morphological info (tense, person, number, gender); lemma (root); and other tokens with various relationships with this one.
- **Entity analysis** identifies named entities in the text. These can be famous people, places, dates, organisations, works of art and so on. The returned list is ordered by "salience" scores: the entities most important in the text are shown first.
- **Sentiment analysis** and **entity sentiment analysis** identify the writer's attitude using a score (indicating how positive or negative the attitude is) and a magnitude (indicating the strength of emotion).
- **Content classification** returns a list of content categories that apply to the text. Categories include news, leisure, legal, arts and many others.

AutoML Natural Language lets you train new, custom versions of the models behind the Natural Language API, based on your own data.
- **Custom entity extraction** involves training the entity analysis algorithm to identify entities and names which are specific to your domain.
- **Custom sentiment analysis** calibrates attitudes to match the sentiment scores shown in your own data.
- **Custom content classification** includes your own unique categories.

The **Video Intelligence API** lets you use an existing model that can describe what happens in a video.

- The model recognises objects, places and actions shown in a video you provide. It uses a classification model with a predefined set of labels.
- It can also detect text that appear in the video using an Optical Character Recognition (OCR) technique.
- It can suggest whether the video contains explicit content, such as adult material or violence.
- Another feature suggests the identity of celebrity faces that appear in the video.
- Tracking is an additional feature, different from identifying or recognising items. Identification is a classification problem that attaches a label to the entire frame, whereas object tracking focuses on motion, and returns a location in the frame (**bounding box**) and the relevant **timestamp**.
- The videos you analyse with the API can be either stored in GCP or streamed.
- You can use the API to transcribe speech and generate automated subtitles (currently in English only).

AutoML Video Intelligence helps you create a custom model, where video contents can be classified with your own labels.

- This service has two separate capabilities: one that **classifies video segments** into categories you define, and another one that **tracks objects** as they move.
- To train a model that identifies your own categories or tracks your objects in videos, you need to provide labelled data including the bounding box and timestamp that each label applies to.
- You can work either in "multi-class" mode, which suggests one label per video segment, or in "multi-label" mode, which can suggest multiple classes for the same video segment.

AutoML Tables lets you build and deploy ML models using data stored as tables in BigQuery and Cloud Storage.

- There is no coding involved. You provide the source tables and the labels that the model should learn to predict. AutoML then

automates the process of exploring your data to find the features that would work best as variables in your model.
- AutoML detect missing values and outliers, and decides the best way to take care of them.
- You can work with this service via the AutoML API, or interactively in a notebook-style env, or via a UI. When you use the UI, it includes some guidance on the end-to-end ML lifecycle and explains model behaviour.
- You can view a range of evaluation metrics from the training process, to learn about the strengths and weaknesses of the model that AutoML has suggested.
- Once you're happy with the model, AutoML Tables lets you deploy it so that it is available either as a service for online requests or for use in batch jobs.
- AutoML Tables is currently in a Beta release.

Dialogflow is the GCP platform for building **conversational UIs**, which you can include in a **chatbot** or in other apps.
- Dialogflow belongs in the wider field of **natural language understanding** (NLU). The challenge for conversational UIs and bots is to deal with the nuances of human dialogue.
- Input to Dialogflow can be either text or audio. The output it produces can be either text or synthetic speech.
- A Dialogflow **agent** is a virtual entity you create so that it can talk to your users.
- The **intent** is what a user wants to achieve in each step ("turn") of the conversation. The intent needs to be structured in a way the agent understands.
- Each agent has a set of intents they know how to deal with. When all these intents are combined, they should allow the agent to handle a full conversation that meets your objectives.
- An intent in Dialogflow is defined by the following elements:
    - ▶ **Training phrases** (things the user might say)
    - ▶ **Action** (what the agent should do)
    - ▶ **Parameters** (to further specify the required action)

- ▶ **Responses** (may include answers, questions, error messages, confirmation).
- To identify the right intent, chatbots often apply a classification model (p131) to user expressions. Dialogflow has a built-in ML model that expands the list of training phrases per intent, so that more user expressions can be understood.
- A **context** is needed to link the current step of a conversation to earlier steps. A context is just a variable that holds the current state of the conversation, or helps determine that some intents are only possible in certain states.
- Applying an "input context" to an intent tells Dialogflow to match the intent only if the context is active.
- Applying an "output context" to an intent tells Dialogflow to activate a context after the intent is matched.
- For example, you can create a conversation where the training phase "show me a picture" returns a dog picture if the context is "likes dogs", or a cat if the context is "likes cats".
- If the agent asks a question, the question itself is activated as a context. This helps interpret the answer correctly.
- You can make the context expire after some time has passed.
- Dialogflow provides predefined "follow-up intents" with matching contexts, to handle common user inputs like "yes" or "no". You can create follow-up intents for other replies.
- Dialogflow integrates with popular conversation platforms (e.g. Google Assistant, Slack, Facebook Messenger) and NLU platforms (e.g. Alexa, Cortana). It knows how to deal with the front end and formatting requirements of each platform, so that you can focus on the unique requirements of your agent.
- In the settings of your intents, you can allow a conversation to trigger a **fulfilment**. This way you can, for example, check a database or call the endpoint of another service ("webhook").

Cloud Speech-to-Text is the GCP speech recognition service.
- The service offers 3 different speech recognition methods.
- The first option is **Synchronous Recognition**. Audio data of up to 1 minute is sent to the Speech-to-Text API; it returns results after all audio has been processed. Then you can send more audio as separate requests.

- The second option is **Asynchronous Recognition**. Audio data is sent to the API, which initiates a long running operation. You can periodically poll for results.
- The third option is **Streaming Recognition**. This method uses a bi-directional stream, for continuous use in real time.
- For synchronous and async recognition, you can send API requests either using the common REST method or Google's gRPC (p27). Streaming recognition only accepts gRPC.
- The requests you send contain audio data and config parameters such as the audio encoding type, sample rate, language and result filtering.
- You can also choose which ML model will be used to transcribe your audio file. The different models are for different types of input: audio in video clips; phone calls; verbal instructions; or a default model for anything else. Each model is available in a different set of languages and has a different cost.
- The response is a JSON file with transcripts for each audio segment, and confidence levels per transcript. Some of the methods produce interim results, which may change as processing continues. There is a "stability" field, which indicates whether results are still likely to change.

Cloud Text-to-Speech converts text to audio files containing speech that mimics a human voice.
- It is for use in apps or bots that speak to the user rather than send written messages. Your app generates messages as it would normally do, and contacts the Text-to-Speech API to convert them to spoken text before responding to the user.
- Over 180 different voices are available, across 30+ languages.
- It can communicate with your app using REST or gRPC.
- The service implements the WaveNet ML model from DeepMind to produce natural-sounding speech.
- In the text you can add tags that add pauses, pronunciation instructions, and rules for date and time formatting.
- You can also control the speed, pitch and volume of produced speech.

7.5 Services for specific sectors

Some GCP services were designed for the needs of specific business sectors or types of organisations.

Cloud IoT Core is a group of GCP services for use in **Internet of Things** (IoT) systems.
- IoT systems include devices such as sensors, mechanical controllers, home appliances and others. Often the compute and data storage capabilities of such devices are limited. Their network connectivity may be intermittent. They are seen as an IoT system if their operation involves some degree of remote operation and collection of telemetry into a central database.
- IoT Core offers two-way communication with IoT devices. One direction is for telemetry and data collection from devices; the other direction allows a central admin function to install updates to the device firmware without involving the user.
- It's worth noting that unless you require this two-way info flow, you can manage a fleet of IoT devices with other GCP services than IoT Core. Data can be streamed from devices directly to a warehouse, database, Cloud Dataflow or Pub/Sub.
- A key component of IoT Core is the **device manager**. This is where you register devices so you can configure them and monitor their work. It's a managed service that also helps with device authentication, authorisation and metadata storage.
- Devices connect to GCP using a **protocol bridge**. IoT Core offers two alternative bridges. The **HTTP bridge** uses the web's most common protocol, and therefore may benefit from wider compatibility. The alternative **MQTT bridge**, based on the MQTT protocol, is more specifically designed for lightweight, "publish subscribe" style exchange of messages in machine-to-machine communications.
- IoT Core doesn't charge you per device, only for the data flow to and from your devices.

Zync is a **3D rendering** service on GCP.
- "Rendering" means producing an image from a file.
- Zync is for situations where you have geometric models of 3D shapes in many different files (e.g. OBJ, FBX and Alembic);

you want to convert them into one large library, with consistent settings and labels, which can be used to train a ML model to recognise these shapes.
- The shapes (**assets**) can be, for example, components produced in a factory.
- Zync renders each asset in an identical env based on preset templates (**rigs**).

Cloud Talent Solution is a job search service with ML features. It provides job search results that go beyond the typical keyword-based search. It is an API with client libraries in several languages, so that job search features can be added in various apps and websites.

The **Cloud Life Sciences API** is a service for the bioinformatics sector, to handle genomics and biomedical data.
- This service is mainly a "wrapper" around various GCP services such as GCE, GCS, BigQuery, IAM and others. The API makes the capabilities of these features more accessible to customers who speak the bioinformatics jargon.
- Some data pipeline development tools and workflow engines are in common use in the life sciences community. These include, for example, Cromwell, Nextflow and Galaxy. The Cloud Life Sciences API makes it easy to run these tools in containers on GCE instances.
- This allows scientists to use tools they are familiar with while also benefiting from the scalability of GCP resources and from easy integration with other GCP services – for example for storage, analysis and ML.

The **Cloud Healthcare API** is tailored for GCP users in the health sector.
- This API, too, is a "wrapper" around other GCP services, such as GKE and BigQuery, which are relevant for common requirements in healthcare management systems.
- By offering users in the health sector this dedicated wrapper, GCP can use sector-specific terminology while still relying on

the same cloud infrastructure for data ingestion, integration, storage, analysis and ML.
- The Healthcare API is compatible with common protocols, formats and standard of the health industry. These include Digital Imaging and Communications in Medicine (**DICOM**), Health Level 7 version 2 (**HL7v2**), and Fast Healthcare Interoperability Resources (**FHIR**).
- The API offers three different **modalities** based on these three standards - DICOM, HL7v2 and FHIR. Each one of these modalities follows a different format and structure for organising your resources.
- Google's proposed way of using the API also gives a key role to Cloud Pub/Sub (p47). The Pub/Sub concept aligns well with the common use case where new medical info about a patient, which has just become available, needs to trigger updates in multiple remote systems.
- Integration with Cloud IAM (p178) is also important to this API. It helps ensure, for example, that electronic protected health information (**ePHI**) and other forms of personally identifiable info (PII) (p201) are stored and processed in a way that complies with regulatory requirements.
- Google maintain a list of GCP services that meet the requirements of laws and standards for security and data protection, including the health industry HIPAA (p201) and the wider ISO/IEC 27001 (p201). The Cloud Healthcare API and many related GCP services are on the list, but it is critical to note that the responsibility for compliance remains with you. GCP gives you tools that can be used in a compliant way, and supporting techniques such as encryption and key management (p188), but your solutions might still be non-compliant if your workflows and solution components don't implement these in a secure way.

Chapter 8
Networking services

8.1 Virtual private cloud

When you use GCP as the provider of managed services (p6) or serverless ones (p7), network settings are hidden and you only have some limited config to do. But if you manage your own cloud infrastructure using GCP resources, it's your responsibility to set up networking arrangements.

A **virtual private cloud** (**VPC**) is a software-defined network that uses Google infrastructure, but has clear boundaries and rules which you define.

- Your VPC is a **unicast** network, where each resource has a private IPv4 (p8) address which can be used for communication with other GCP resources and services. Internal traffic can't use IPv6 (p8).
- Typical resources to connect using a VPC include GCE VMs (p33), GKE clusters (p52), and GAE Flex instances (p44).
- Traffic within a VPC stays inside Google's private network, but it leaves this network when communicating with end users.
- If you use the **standard network tier**, your traffic exits the Google network close to your GCP resources. The remaining journey to the end user is done on the internet.
- If you use the **premium network tier**, your traffic exits the Google network close to the user or the destination. So the part that uses the internet is shorter, which gives you lower latency and better security.
- The standard tier is mainly for cost minimisers who don't host critical systems on GCP. Various GCP services are only available with the premium tier (e.g. global load balancing or CDN), so heavy GCP users need the premium tier.
- VPC networks, including their routes and firewall rules, are **global** resources, not associated with any region or zone. This is different from VPCs in AWS.

- The VPC network itself doesn't have a range of IPs.
- A VPC must have at least one **subnet**. Subnets are **regional**.
- VMs are created in a specific VPC, in a specific subnet, in a specific **zone**.
- You create the VM from a template which is global.
- MIGs (p36) can be created either in a region or a zone.
- Kubernetes container clusters are created in a specific region or a zone, in a specific subnet.
- Each subnet has a range of IPs.
  - ▶ When you create a subnet, you define its range of IPs, using the convention known as a **CIDR block**.
  - ▶ You must define a primary range, but you can also optionally add a secondary one. The secondary range would be used only for **alias IPs**. You use aliases, for example, for VPC-native GKE clusters (p57).
  - ▶ The benefit of having a secondary range of IPs is that the two ranges cannot mix, so you can separate VMs from container-based services, and have different settings (e.g. firewalls) for each use.
  - ▶ Every subnet has four reserved IPs in the primary range. They are reserved for the following purposes: one for use as the address of the network itself; one for the default internet gateway (p147); one for broadcast traffic; and one address is kept by Google for potential future use.
- GCP offers two network modes, which vary in the way subnets are created -
  - ▶ An **auto mode** VPC comes with one subnet ready to use in each region. You can add more subnets manually.
  - ▶ A **custom mode** VPC is created without subnets.
  - ▶ Auto mode networks can be later converted to custom, but not vice versa.
  - ▶ Unless you disable the relevant org policy (p24), each new project starts with a default network in auto mode.
  - ▶ The subnets of any auto mode network use the same range of internal addresses. So you can't connect auto mode networks to each other, due to address conflicts.
- Each VM is connected to a subnet using a **network interface**. By default, it only connects to one subnet in one VPC, but you

145

can add interfaces to subnets in other VPCs. In such cases, the same VM will be directly connected to more than one network. This may help if the VM provides a service to these networks, but the networks themselves should remain disconnected.

- Each interface needs an internal IP address, and it can also have an external one. You can't use two interfaces to connect a VM to the same VPC.
- VPC **Flow Logs** record network traffic flows sent or received by VMs, including instances used as GKE nodes.
  - ▶ You can use the logs for network monitoring, incident investigation, security analysis or cost optimisation.
  - ▶ The logs can be streamed to Cloud Pub/Sub if you want to undertake analysis in real time.
  - ▶ Each subnet can have Flow Logs enabled or disabled. If enabled, logs are collected from all VMs in the subnet.
  - ▶ The logging mechanism is a native element of the VPC infrastructure, so there is no performance impact.
  - ▶ TCP and UDP traffic (p9) is logged. It is sent to Cloud Logging (p208) and stored there for 30 days. You can use filters to exclude some of it or to export to another destination, such as longer-term storage. Flow Logs don't work at the HTTP request level.
  - ▶ Data traffic is made of small data **packets**. About 1 packet in 10 is captured for logging purposes, but it can vary with the VM load. This setting isn't adjustable.
  - ▶ Flow Logs aggregates packets into one log entry per time interval. Intervals can vary from 5 seconds to 15 minutes.
  - ▶ You can also choose to only send a sample of logs. The default sample rate is 50%.
  - ▶ Each flow record includes base fields and metadata. Metadata fields may be omitted to save storage costs. The log includes some multi-fields, with more than one piece of data in one field. For example, the IP address, port and protocol of both source and destination are all in one field.
- VPCs don't have a direct cost; you pay for the resources you use in the VPC. You also pay for the volume of your logs.

- VPCs have evolved from GCP **legacy networks**. Google recommend that you avoid using legacy networks, but existing ones are still partially supported. Legacy networks have a single range of IPs, which can't be divided into subnets. IPs in this range can be spread unpredictably across regions.

8.2 VPC routes

Applicable routes define what paths data can take when it leaves a VM, no matter what's in the data or where it goes.
- Each VPC has a **virtual routing table**. This table is a managed service: you are responsible for defining the routes, but the table itself is distributed and scalable resource. Changes to the routing table are "eventually consistent" (p7).
- Each data packet has a specified destination. Each route is defined by a **destination** and a **next hop**. Packets to a specific destination can be sent from their current location to a specific address if there is a route that allows data to this destination to make this hop.
- If a VM acts as a next hop, its settings need to allow IP forwarding. In the firewall rules (p149) of this VM, the "source" and "destination" refer to the source and destination of the packet. The VM itself isn't a source or a destination.
- Your **default internet gateway** is an instance in your network which has access to external IPs. You define this gateway as the next hop for traffic with public IPs.
- Routing doesn't consider geographical distance. If your next hop is far away, it will affect cost and latency.
- In the definition of a route, the destination can be a range of IPs. Ranges may overlap, so a specific destination may be covered by multiple routes.
- There are three general routes categories–
  - ▶ **System-generated default routes**. They define paths to allow VMs to access the internet and internal resources. They can be deleted or replaced with a customer route.
  - ▶ **System-generated subnet routes**. They define paths to allow traffic between subnets. Subnet routes are global and can't be deleted.
  - ▶ **Custom routes**. You use these to allow traffic to any destination you wish – for example, a specific VM in a

subnet, or a range of IPs that is broader than a single subnet. You can use network tags (p22) to filter VMs.

- **Custom** routes can take one of these three modes -
  - ▶ With **static routing**, the next hop can be a specific instance name, an IP address or a VPN tunnel. Static routes are global. GCP doesn't let you create a static route with a more specific destination than any subnet route.
  - ▶ With **regional dynamic routing**, Cloud Routers (p168) in your VPC share their routes with other networks they're connected to via VPN (p170) or Interconnect (p172), within the same region. If you choose dynamic routing, the regional option is the default.
  - ▶ With **global dynamic routing**, Cloud Routers in your VPC share their routes with connected networks in any region.
- To fully define which route traffic should take, routes get **priorities**. Some priorities are assigned automatically by GCP while others are for you to decide.
  - ▶ The route with the highest priority is selected if available.
  - ▶ Subnet routes have built-in, auto precedence.
  - ▶ A subnet route gets a higher priority than a dynamic route if the subnet route covers a wider range of destinations.
  - ▶ A static route gets a higher priority than a dynamic route if their ranges of destinations are equally wide.
  - ▶ Between custom routes with the same specific destination, the local network and static routes get a higher priority.
  - ▶ Between dynamic routes, those advertised by a Cloud Router get a higher priority.
  - ▶ When a static route has a VM or VPN tunnel as the next hop, GCP will choose it even when it causes errors. A dynamic route that causes errors is just ignored.
- When traffic leaves a VM to a destination it isn't directly connected to, the default **destination-based routing policy** sends it via the VM's primary interface. You can change to a **source-based routing policy** if you want traffic to be sent via interfaces of a peered network (p151).
- Routes to and from a load balancer work differently. See section 8.5.

8.3 Firewalls

A virtual, software-defined **firewall** in each VPC lets you control what data traffic you allow into your network ("ingress"), out of it ("egress") or in the network. You do this using **firewall rules**.

- Every VPC has two "implied firewall rules". They block all incoming traffic and allow all outgoing traffic. You can't delete these rules but you can override them.
- The default network of your project has additional rules, allowing internal traffic. These rules are optional in other networks.
- Firewall rules are **stateful**, i.e. they have a memory. Once a connection has started and at least one message has been sent, the firewall will accept a response. This is the case for both ingress and egress traffic. A session is considered active if at least one data packet is sent every 10 minutes.
- Each firewall rule includes -
  - ▶ The **target** (a VM in the VPC, or the whole VPC, or resources with specific tags, or specific service accounts)
  - ▶ The **source** (for ingress traffic)
  - ▶ The **destination** (for egress traffic)
  - ▶ A **priority** (a small number means a higher priority)
  - ▶ **Direction** of traffic (ingress or egress)
  - ▶ **Enforcement status** (rule enabled or disabled)
  - ▶ **Protocol**
  - ▶ **Port**
  - ▶ **Action** (allow or deny)
- The source and destination can be inside or outside the VPC. They can be defined by an IP range and further filtered by network tags (p22) or service accounts (p181), but not both.
- Unlike routing decisions, in firewall rules the highest priority wins, no matter if it's less specific than a low-priority rule.
- Unlike routes, you can't share firewall rules among networks, even if they are peered (p151) or connected with VPN.
- Whatever the firewall rules, GCP only allows the TCP, UDP, ICMP and IPIP protocols for external traffic. The GRE protocol is blocked even internally. Egress SMTP traffic is blocked too.

- Instances can always access the GCP metadata server, which provides various services including DHCP (allocation of IPs and other config info), NTP (Network Time Protocol), and DNS (matching IPs to domains).
- A firewall isn't the only way to filter traffic by port; you can use forwarding rules (p153), for example. But firewall rules should be a primary port filtering method. They are designed as a security mechanism, while forwarding rules aren't.
- To have access to the internet, a VM needs the following –
  - ▶ Firewall rules allowing egress traffic
  - ▶ A valid default internet gateway route (p147), or a custom route with the widest destination IP range (0.0.0.0/0)
  - ▶ An external IP address, or access to Cloud NAT (p167), or access to a VM which acts as a proxy with external access.
- **Firewall rules logging** allows you to view and analyse the effects of your firewall rules –
  - ▶ You can enable logging individually for each firewall rule.
  - ▶ If enabled, a "connection record" is created each time the rule allows or denies traffic. The record contains the source and destination IPs, protocol, ports, date, time, firewall reference and "disposition" (allowed/denied).
  - ▶ You can export these connection records to Cloud Logging, Cloud Pub/Sub or BigQuery for analysis.
  - ▶ Only TCP and UDP connections can be logged.
  - ▶ You can't log the "implied" rules and lowest-priority rules.
  - ▶ There are limits on how many connections you can log per machine type (p33).

8.4 Network sharing and peering

A **Shared VPC** is a network that can be used from more than one project in one org.
- Projects sharing a VPC can communicate using internal IPs.
- A network is shared when a **host project** gives access to its networks to one or more **service projects**.
- Networks in service projects are not shared with the host.

- A service project can only be attached to one host project, and can't have its own service projects.
- When a host project is enabled, all of its existing VPCs become shared. Resources that existed in a service project before it was attached to the host can't use the shared network.
- The host and service projects don't share their external IPs.
- Static internal IPs (p166) need to be created in the project where they'll be used, although the address itself will come from the range of available IPs in a shared subnet.
- VMs in the same service project can reach each other using the internal DNS names that GCP gives them. These names use the ID of the service project where the VMs are created, even though they point to internal IPs in the host project.
- Service projects continue to be billed separately.
- A shared network can connect via VPN to an on-prem network.
- Shared networks can help implement the "**least privilege**" principle, using IAM roles (p179). Some typical scenarios –
  ▶ Org admins delegate limited responsibilities to service project admins
  ▶ A central network team provides an admin function but have no access to the service projects
  ▶ Members of a service project only get access to specific subnets in the host project.
- Deployment Manager (p204) can only manage resources in one project, so using it in a Shared VPC needs a special setup.
- A "standalone project" is one that does not participate in the Shared VPC; it is neither a host nor a service project.

Networks can be **peered** to each other, even in different projects or orgs. The **peer** networks can then connect using private IPs.

- Traffic between the peers stays within Google's network and doesn't traverse the internet. It will have the same latency, throughput, availability and security level as traffic within one network. You also get lower egress prices.
- A network can peer with multiple others (up to a limit).
- The peers exchange all their subnet routes. You can also exchange custom routes (both static and dynamic), if the

network where routes are defined has exported them. This allows networks to learn routes from their peers.

- Network tags and service accounts aren't shared between the peers, so static routes based on these can't be used across peered networks. Static routes where the "next hop" is the default internet gateway aren't shared either.
- The sharing of routes doesn't mean shared route management. Each VPC manages its own routes and VPNs.
- IP ranges of a network must not overlap with those used in a static route in a peer network. Dynamic routes cause less trouble – an overlapping IP range is just ignored.
- Each side of the peering is set up independently.
- Firewall rules are not exchanged between the peers. The rules in each VPC need to allow traffic from VMs in the other.
- You can create a transit network that peers with several networks and provides a central function to all of them. However, Google only allow this if peers always communicate using direct routes. You're not allowed to create a network that traffic just hops through on its way between peers.
- Peering with a shared VPC is allowed. A shared network can have both peers and service projects. Service projects have internal access to peers of the host project.
- When a peered network includes VMs with multiple network interfaces, you need a source-based routing policy (p148).

8.5 Principles of load balancing

When you run a solution on GCP, **Cloud Load Balancing** has an important role in ensuring the scalability and high availability of your solution. This is a managed and auto-scaling service, that distributes incoming traffic across your resources to optimise their reliability.

A load balancer implements the anycast routing concept: a single IP address gives users access to multiple destinations, with auto selection of the most suitable one, for example the one closest to the user. The IP address, together with a port number (p8) and the protocol of incoming traffic, constitute the front end of a service you create in a VPC. The load balancer allows you to associate a **forwarding rule** with this front end, so that requests don't have to indicate which specific resource at the back end they go to; this can be decided in real time based on the condition of your network.

The load balancer and its forwarding rule spread incoming traffic across available backends (p8). Every backend has an associated **health check**, which the load balancer uses to verify that the backend accepts new requests.
- Only healthy backends will receive traffic. If a backend fails the check, the load balancer is responsible for automatic failover to a healthy one.
- When the backends are in a MIG (p36), the health checks can also trigger auto-healing.
- The health check involves sending a request to the backend, and seeing the backend as healthy if it sends back the expected response. Every such attempt is called a **probe**.
- The probe might come from various IPs, so backends need firewall rules allowing traffic from the relevant range of IPs.
- By default, you'd send this request using the same protocol that the load balancer deals with (for example, an HTTP probe from an HTTP load balancer). You can use other protocols - HTTP(S), SSL or TCP - but not UDP. Backends that use UDP need to allow TCP for the health check.
- You'd usually send the health check to the same port that the load balancer uses.
- When creating health checks, you specify the "check interval" and "timeout", or accept the default values of 5 seconds. But if multiple addresses or forwarding rules point to the same backend, it might get checked more frequently.
- HTTP(S) checks are successful if the response is a 200 code. Other checks are happy with any response, but you can use a "content-based" check, which requires a specific response.
- SSL and TCP checks also require completion of a handshake.

Since load balancers split incoming traffic across different backends, **session affinity** is a big issue. Session affinity is important when traffic comes from a client (e.g. a user) that has already started communicating with a specific backend instance, and may already have some parameters stored on that instance.

If the load balancer forwards later messages from the same client to a different backend, it could cause a mess.
- Cloud Load Balancing uses session affinity, but not always. The points here are general; see more specific detail later.
- The session affinity setting determines how the load balancer decides which backend instance to send traffic to. You choose which parameters will define a "session". Once you've configured what counts as one session, the load balancer can ensure that all traffic that belongs to the same session is sent to the same backend instance.
- Parameters that may be used to define a session include the client's IP address, the request's protocol, the port number, and whether or not the request includes a "cookie" file created when the session started. The choice of parameters from this list varies between the different types of GCP load balancers.
- If sessions are defined by multiple parameters, then only requests that share all these parameters will be routed to the same instance. This gives the load balancer more flexibility to balance all other traffic between healthy backends, without being constrained by a strict definition of a session.
- Defining a session only by the client's IP, or using a cookie attached to every request, will maximise the consistent matching of requests to backends, but it will give the load balancer less freedom to do its balancing work.
- Session affinity can be lost in various scenarios – for example, if the instance that serves a session becomes unhealthy, or runs out of capacity, or gets removed by auto-scaling.

Traffic routing to and from load balancers is different from routing (p147) elsewhere in GCP. This applies to the main traffic between the load balancer and your VMs, and also to health checking traffic: these routes are not controlled by the VPC.

Before I continue presenting the different services GCP includes under the title Cloud Load Balancing, it's important to note that GCP also offers load balancing as part of other services, even if it's not in the title. **Table 10** reviews the load balancing features of different GCP services.

Table 10: GCP services with load balancing features

Service	What it does to balance load
MIG	Requests are distributed so that workload is spread across healthy instances, even if you don't use Cloud Load Balancing.
GCF	GCF is serverless, so load balancing across the resources it runs your function on is fully managed.
GAE	The auto-scaling behaviour can implicitly handle cases of imbalanced load.
Cloud Pub/Sub	Data centre load is considered when Pub/Sub decides where to store newly arriving messages. Within each data centre, messages are distributed across different forwarders, to reduce latency.
Cloud Tasks	High workload is handled by storing tasks in a queue and performing them asynchronously.
GKE	Container-native load balancing (p57) with NEGs (p158) is a feature of Cloud Load Balancing. Alternatively, manually adding a Kubernetes Ingress (p58) object creates an HTTP(S) load balancer (p160) that you can use to distribute traffic across multiple groups of backend services. A more basic form of load balancing is performed when using any of GKE's auto-scalers (p54).
Istio	Istio has several options for load balancing across backends, with a rich set of features.
Traffic Director	Many of the HTTP(S) Load Balancing features are available in Traffic Director as a managed service, including a global endpoint.
Anthos	For cloud-based parts of your Anthos solution you can combine the load balancing features of Cloud Load Balancing and GKE. The on-prem parts can integrate with a traditional load balancer.
Cloud Load Balancing	See section 8.6.

155

8.6 Types of load balancing

Under the title Cloud Load Balancing, GCP currently offers 6 different services. You can group them in several different ways:
- By the **protocol** they serve – HTTP(S), SSL, TCP, UDP.
- By the **source** of traffic – internal to GCP or external.
- By the **geography** of the resources they help keep in balance – global or regional.
- By whether they act as a **proxy** or just pass traffic through.

The types of GCP load balancers are shown in **table 11**. "LB" is used in the table instead of "Load Balancing". Note that the network load balancing services are listed more than once.

Table 11: services included in Cloud Load Balancing

Source *Protocol*	**Internal traffic**	**External traffic**
HTTP(S)	Internal HTTP(S) LB	External HTTP(S) LB
SSL	-	External SSL Proxy LB
TCP	Internal TCP/UDP LB	External TCP/UDP LB External TCP Proxy LB
UDP	Internal TCP/UDP LB	External TCP/UDP LB

The HTTP(S) load balancers (internal and external) don't have "proxy" in the name, but they are proxies just like the SSL Proxy and TCP Proxy. So 4 of the 6 load balancing services are proxies. Google use the term "proxy" here for what is more commonly known as "reverse proxy". A load balancer is a (reverse) **proxy** if, together with the forwarding rule (p153), it acts as your client-facing front end.

Your clients send their traffic to the proxy since some details of the services behind it are hidden. The proxy terminates the connection with the client and opens a separate one with your own backends. The proxy replaces the source IP address with its own address. So a proxy load balancer intervenes quite significantly in your traffic. Proxy load balancers also have other functions, such as decrypting encrypted messages.

The alternative to a proxy is what Google describe as a **pass-through** load balancer. The TCP/UDP load balancers (internal and external) work this way: they are not presented to clients as a front end, and they don't hide the backend from clients. Their role is somewhat more basic than proxy load balancers. They don't have additional roles other than load balancing; for example, they don't allow communication using IPv6 addresses.

Another important difference between proxy and pass-through load balancing is in the way backends send responses to clients. When there's a proxy load balancer, backends respond to the client via the load balancer; with a pass-through load balancer, the backend responds directly to the client. This feature of pass-through load balancers is sometimes called "direct server return".

The external proxy load balancers (HTTP(S), SSL, TCP) are based on the Google Front End (**GFE**) technology. GFEs are located at Google's network edge locations (p15). If you use any of the 3 GFE load balancers with the premium network tier (p144), you can deploy these load balancers as **global** resources. This works well when you create backends in different regions and you want to allow simple access to any of them, using only one global IP address. The global load balancers can direct every request to the healthy backend that is closest to the user.

The GFE load balancers (external HTTP(S), SSL and TCP proxies) are the only ones that let you communicate with clients using IPv6 (p8). These load balancers can have both IPv4 and IPv6 external addresses; they need separate forwarding rules, but can link both to the same load balancer. When they terminate the external connection, the internal one they create with the backends is based on IPv4 only. The IPv6 connection is resumed when the load balancer receives a response from the backend and sends it over IPv6 to the external client.

When using the standard network tier, or any of the internal load balancers, or any of the TCP/UDP load balancers, load balancing is **regional**. This works well when your resources and your clients are in a single region, and you need load balancing across backends that may span all zones in the region.

Most load balancing options (all except External TCP/UDP) distinguish between the "backend" and the "backend service".
- The **backend service** is a service provided by the load balancer and defined in the load balancing config.
- The backend service directs traffic to **backends**.
- These terms can easily confuse, because the backends themselves provide services, but the term "backend service" doesn't refer to them.
- Backends can be any of the following:
    - ▶ MIGs (p36)
    - ▶ Unmanaged instance groups (p36)
    - ▶ Network endpoint groups (NEGs) (see below).
- You can associate managed and unmanaged instance groups with the same backend service.
- You can't associate instance groups and NEGS with the same backend service.
- With HTTP(S), you can have multiple backend services behind one load balancer.
- With SSL, TCP and UDP, you can only have one backend service per load balancer.
- Cloud Load balancing doesn't keep your backend instances in sync. If you set up a load balancer to spread traffic between instances, it's your responsibility to ensure that this doesn't cause conflict or data inconsistency.

A combination of an IP address and a port number is called a **network endpoint**. A collection of network endpoints in a single subnet is called a **network endpoint group** or **NEG**.
- NEGs are an alternative to instance groups. They can be used as the backend behind any external proxy load balancer.
- For each request, the load balancer picks one endpoint from the NEG and sends the traffic there.
- The importance of NEGs is that they extend the concept of load balancing to also include load balancing across GKE pods (p52). This approach, also called **container-native load**

balancing, relies on the ability to give individual IPs to GKE pods and containerised services.
- NEGs are zonal resources, and can only be used in the zone where the endpoints are.
- You can also create a NEG implicitly, from the GKE side, by letting the Ingress controller (p58) do the work for you.
- Endpoints on one VM can be in one NEG or in different NEGs.
- NEGs can't point to public IPs.

Each of the load balancing services has one or more **balancing mode** options. The balancing mode determines how the backend service distributes traffic to backends. The most basic balancing mode is a "round robin", which loops across instances and sends requests to each instance when its turn comes. But some of the load balancing services have additional balancing modes that use more precise metrics, such as the backend CPU utilisation, rate of requests per second, or the number of connections. Some balancing modes also work with a "capacity" parameter to define a specific target, for example a 85% backend utilisation target.

HTTP(S) and SSL load balancers work with the SSL protocol (p9). You can control some SSL settings using **SSL policies**. Many orgs attach high importance to these settings because they affect the level of security of data sent over the internet.
- To define an SSL policy, you choose a profile, which is a set of pre-configured features.
- There are 3 preset profiles and a custom profile.
- The preset profiles are "compatible" (allows most clients), "modern" (allows newer versions only) and "restricted" (meets stricter criteria).
- In the custom profile you can select SSL features individually (e.g. which SSL versions to allow).
- SSL policies apply to traffic between clients and the proxy, not to traffic between the proxy and the backend.

Let's talk now about some specific characteristics of each of the 6 load balancing services.

External HTTP(S) Load Balancing offers **content-based** mapping of requests to backend services based on the incoming URL.

- You can have multiple backend services behind one load balancer and one IP address. They can span multiple web domains.
- You create a **URL map**, which can route requests to different backend services based on the host name (the domain part of the URL) or the path (the remaining part of the URL).
- In the URL map, the host name is analysed by a **host rule** that uses a **path matcher**. Each path matcher includes a default path and different **path rules**. Each path rule returns a backend service.
- You can't define URL paths dynamically, but some wildcards are allowed in the matcher syntax.
- You can't use a URL map to switch from HTTP to HTTPS. But you can use the same URL map, host rules and path matchers for both HTTP and HTTPs requests, by referencing the URL map by both a target HTTP proxy and a target HTTPS proxy.
- To create an HTTPS load balancer, for example for a payment processing form, you need a dedicated sub-domain (e.g. pay.form.com); an SSL certificate that has been registered for this sub-domain; and valid DNS entries at your web registrar.
- You can use HTTP(S) Load Balancing as the front end of a storage service on GCS (p73). To do this, you choose a default "backend bucket" instead of a default backend service.
- You choose the protocol for communication between the load balancer and the backends - HTTP, HTTPS, or HTTP/2. It then uses only the protocol that you chose, and doesn't fall back to others if your chosen one fails.

Internal HTTP(S) Load Balancing is similar to its external sister. It provides a front end for one or more HTTP(S) backend services.
- The biggest difference is that the IP address of the front end is private. You use this load balancer to distribute traffic when the clients, and not just the services, are internal to your VPC.
- This service is based on the open-source Envoy proxy, not on GFE (p157). It balances load within a region and not globally.
- Like the external HTTP(S) load balancer, the internal one also uses a **URL map** and offers **content-based** load balancing.

- Various GCP services, that work with the external HTTP(S) load balancer, aren't compatible with the internal one. These include Identity-Aware Proxy, Cloud CDN, Cloud Armor, GCS, Google-managed SSL certificates, SSL policies and VPC network peering.

SSL Proxy Load Balancing is for traffic sent over SSL, but not HTTPS.
- It can improve the efficiency of your backend VMs, because it is designed to process SSL. Such processing would be CPU-intensive if not done by a specialised service.
- Using this load balancer means you don't control the locations where SSL connections are terminated, because this is done at all Google network edge locations. If for various reasons (e.g. regulatory requirements) you want to determine where SSL connections are terminated, you should use External TCP/UDP Load Balancing instead, since it is a regional service.
- The SSL Proxy can handle HTTPS, but the HTTP(S) load balancer does it better, because it knows HTTPS versions, has CDN integration, and other HTTPS-specific features.
- The SSL Proxy sends all data from the same connection to the same backend instance, unlike the HTTP(S) Proxy that handles each request separately.
- The SSL Proxy can be used for other protocols sent over SSL, such as WebSocket and IMAP.
- Traffic from the proxy to the backend can use SSL or TCP. The advantage of using SSL also for this leg of the trip is that it gives you end-to-end encryption. The disadvantage is that your backends will need to be able to handle SSL, which is the same thing you were going to avoid by using the SSL proxy.
- External-facing SSL certificates can be either self-managed or Google-managed. If you also use SSL on the backend, you can use self-signed certificates which are easier to manage.

TCP Proxy Load Balancing is for TCP traffic (obviously), but not if it uses HTTP(S) or SSL. These protocols have their own specialised proxies. It's also worth highlighting that external TCP traffic can be load-balanced either with this proxy or with the pass-through, network TCP/UDP load balancer.

External TCP/UDP Load Balancing is more commonly known as **network load balancing**.

- This is a non-proxied, pass-through service, so traffic arrives at your VMs from its original sender and not from the load balancer. This means that your firewall rules need to allow traffic from a much wider range of IPs.
- When backends send responses to clients, they use the external IP address of the load balancer as the source.
- The network load balancer is based on the Andromeda technology for virtual networking and Google's Maglev.
- It uses a different terminology from other load balancers. This is annoying, although the key concepts aren't that different. Instead of instance groups and backend services, network load balancers use **target pools**. A target pool is a group of VMs that receive traffic from the load balancer's forwarding rules.
- You can include one or more instance groups in a target pool, but you can't distribute traffic to containers.
- Network Load Balancing can auto-scale the instance groups in a target pool based on CPU utilisation.
- You can have multiple forwarding rules, with different combinations of IPs, ports and protocols, pointing to the same target pool.
- The network load balancer respects session affinity (p153) settings for TCP traffic, but these settings are less important than with other load balancers, because all packets in the same TCP connection are sent to the same VM anyway. Only new connections get load-balanced, so if your VMs serve long-lived connections, the load balancer might actually not have sufficient opportunity to keep their loads balanced.
- Session affinity doesn't add much value when balancing UDP traffic, since the UDP protocol doesn't support continuity across multiple requests.
- Network Load Balancing uses a legacy, HTTP-based health check (p153), so you need a basic HTTP server on each VM.
- Each load balancer can support TCP or UDP, but not both.
- You can use the network load balancer for SSL traffic, if you don't mind your VMs dealing with decryption and certificates.

Internal TCP/UDP Load Balancing helps distribute traffic across VMs sitting behind one private IP address within one VPC.
- Like its external brother, this load balancer works entirely within one specified region.
- Unlike the external brother, it uses a similar language as most other GCP load balancers. For the backend you can use any instance group – managed or unmanaged, zonal or regional.
- You can use internal and external TCP/UDP load balancers together. The internal one sits behind an external one and serves traffic that has been routed into a specific network.
- The **active pool** is the set of backend VMs that can get new traffic. You can split your instance group into **primary VMs** and **backup VMs**, and define a **failover policy**. The policy defines the **failover ratio** when the load balancer starts using the backup VMs instead of the primary VMs as the active pool.
- You can't use this service with containers and NEGs.
- One load balancer accepts TCP or UDP traffic, but not both.

8.7 Cloud DNS

DNS is the service that network clients (like web browsers) go to when they need to know the IP address behind a "domain name" or "hostname". Domain names or hostnames, such as "www.economo.tech", are used because people can remember them, but it's the IP address that points to the cloud resource.

The IPs that correspond to names are stored in **DNS records**. You can request access to these records from a **name server**. Searching through DNS records is a **DNS lookup**.

Cloud DNS is a managed DNS service on GCP.
- It's a **global**, highly-available service, that offers a 100% uptime guarantee. Lookups are routed to the nearest server.
- A **managed zone** holds DNS records that share the same DNS name suffix (e.g. example.com). A project can have multiple managed zones. All records in a managed zone are hosted on the same name server.
- Note that a "zone" here isn't a location. It's not a GCP zone.
- Cloud DNS offers both public and private managed zones –

- ▶ Records in a public zone are visible to internet users. Your external users will need them in order to access the GCP resources you make public.
- ▶ Records in a private zone are used inside a project only. They store the names of your VMs, load balancers and other GCP resources. These can be your own custom names or names that GCP gives automatically.
- ▶ You can create a "split horizon" config – a mix of public and private zones, which assigns the same domain name to different addresses, depending on who the client is.

■ There's a universal set of DNS record types, and Cloud DNS supports many of them. Important record types include:
- ▶ "A" record (maps a hostname to an IPv4 address)
- ▶ AAAA (maps a hostname to an IPv6 address)
- ▶ CAA (defines a certificate authority)
- ▶ CNAME (lists an alias of the hostname)
- ▶ MX (maps a domain name to a mail exchange server)
- ▶ NS (delegates the DNS lookup to another name server)
- ▶ PTR (lists a pointer record, for use in reverse lookups where you map an IP address to a name)

■ Cloud DNS allows you to have **overlapping zones**, like in the case of dev.gcp.example.com and gcp.example.com. However, they are only allowed if they are on different name servers. This can be done, for example, in different VPCs. An example of why you might want such overlap is when you want your different testing envs to be consistently named.

■ **DNS peering** lets you ("DNS producer") authorise another network ("DNS consumer") to do DNS lookups in your private zone. It's a one-way relationship. You often introduce DNS peering because you use VPC peering. DNS peering isn't automatically triggered by VPC peering; you do it separately.

■ **DNS forwarding** happens when a DNS lookup is received in one DNS zone and sent to another zone where the relevant DNS records can be found.
- ▶ Two-way forwarding can be set up using "DNS server policies", for example between a VPC and an on-prem data centre connected with Cloud VPN (p170).

- ▶ One-way forwarding can be set up from a "forwarding zone" to any target zone. The forwarding zone is a managed private zone with no DNS records. You set it up so that it can forward DNS lookups from its private env to wherever the relevant DNS records are found.
- You can create **subdomains** by simply adding "A" records or other DNS records in the managed zone of the parent domain. Alternatively, in public zones only, you can "delegate" a subdomain to a different zone using an NS records.
- Public zones support the DNS security extensions (DNSSEC) to improve the authentication of DNS lookups.

8.8 IP addresses

We spoke a lot about IPs already. Let's tidy up a few things.
- When creating VMs, if you don't specify a primary IP address, GCE assigns one automatically. In an auto mode network (p145), the address comes from the IP range of the subnet. In a custom mode network (p145), you must specify which subnet the IP address will come from.
- Each VM instance can have -
  - ▶ One **primary internal** IP address
  - ▶ One or more **secondary internal** IPs
  - ▶ One **external** IP address.
- The above assumes that the VM is in one VPC. If the VM is connected to multiple networks, each connection uses a separate **network interface**. Each network interface will have one internal IP address and potentially one external address.
- Secondary internal addresses can be used if multiple apps, services or GKE pods are running in the VM, and you want them to have separate IPs. These IPs come from the range of alias internal IPs.
- Forwarding rules (p153) for load balancing have IPs, too. These IPs are internal or external, based on the load balancing service you use.
- Addresses can be either ephemeral or static -
  - ▶ **Static** IPs have to be reserved from the available range. They can be registered with DNS and domain providers. They remain attached to a resource and to a project until they're explicitly released, even if the resource is deleted.

- ▶ **Static external** IPs can be either **regional** or **global**. The global ones are used for global forwarding rules only.
- ▶ **Ephemeral** IPs are assigned automatically and randomly. Ephemeral **internal** IPs remain attached to a resource until the resource is deleted, whereas ephemeral **external** IPs remain attached only until the resource is stopped or terminated; then they are released.
- ▶ There's no direct way to tell whether an IP address is static or ephemeral after it has been assigned to a resource. Indirectly, you can search for the address in the list of static external IPs reserved to that project.
- When a VM has an internal address only –
  - ▶ It can still access the public IPs of Google services if you turn on the **Private Google Access** setting for the relevant subnet. The VM will use the default route (p147) that has a "next hop" to the default internet gateway (p147).
  - ▶ It can also use **Private Services Access** to connect to services offered by either Google or third-parties ("service producers") via internal IPs. GCP implements these connections by peering your VPC and the service producer's VPC (p151).
  - ▶ It can connect to GAE Standard (p43) or GCF (p42) services in the same project using **serverless VPC access**. This creates a "connector" with an internal address in the VPC.
- IPv4 addresses have both regional and global quotas.
- "In-use" IPs include any IPs that are being used by a resource. They've so far not incurred charges, only static unused ones. From 2020 all external IPs are charged, whether or not they're in-use, although those in-use still cost less.

8.9 Cloud NAT

NAT servers provide network address translation: they help devices without external IPs connect to the internet. **Cloud NAT** is the GCP version, providing a NAT service to VMs and private GKE clusters.
- It is a managed, software-defined, auto-scaling, highly available service. It adjusts itself to your traffic volumes.
- It's a *regional* resource. You might need a Cloud NAT in each region of each of your networks.
- You can configure it to allow traffic from all or just some of the IP ranges of subnets in a region.
- It implements NAT for connections that start in your VPC. For these connections, Cloud NAT translates between internal and external IPs for both outbound traffic and the inbound response. But it doesn't offer this service to inbound traffic which wasn't initiated inside your network.
- In GKE, both nodes and pods can use Cloud NAT.
- You typically apply a pool of IPs and/or port numbers to the NAT service, so that it can handle many connections.
    - ▶ It is recommended to let GCP auto-allocate IPs for NAT.
    - ▶ Cloud NAT does **endpoint-independent mapping** of outbound traffic. When your VMs connect to external destinations using the same source IP address and port number, this traffic will always be allocated the same IP and port, even if the destinations aren't the same.
    - ▶ Cloud NAT does **endpoint-dependent filtering** of inbound traffic. Responses from the internet are allowed through only if they are from an IP address and port number that you previously contacted.
    - ▶ The number of ports available to Cloud NAT determines the maximum number of simultaneous connections you can have with one external destination.
    - ▶ When you use Cloud NAT with the primary IP range of a subnet, GCP automatically enables Private Google Access (p166) for that subnet.
    - ▶ When you enable NAT for a GKE node, you need to allow it to use all IP ranges of the subnet, with all containers. Each node is allocated a certain number of ports.

- Cloud NAT traffic isn't really sent via a gateway or a proxy. Under the hood, each VM is given a range of IPs and ports to use, and it then communicates with its external destination without mediation.
- NAT config is not imported to a peered network.
- Cloud NAT is not used in the following cases, even if you have configured it: if your VMs or GKE nodes have external IPs; if the backend is behind a load balancer; if your destination is a Google service; if you override your **default internet gateway** next hop with a custom route; or if you create a custom static route whose next hop is a **Cloud VPN tunnel**.

8.10 Cloud Router

When a network on GCP has a **VPN** connection (p170) to an on-prem network, **Cloud Router** can be used to dynamically exchange routes between them.

- Cloud Router creates a peering relationship with your on-prem VPN gateway or router.
- It's a managed, distributed, auto-scaling service.
- Each Cloud Router belongs to a specific VPC and **region**.
- The use of Cloud Router is free. You pay for the amount of traffic it serves but not for the router itself.
- Without Cloud Router –
    - ▶ Routing is static. The only possible routes in your network are those defined explicitly in your **routing table** (p147).
    - ▶ If a link fails, traffic can only be re-routed as per the routes in the table.
    - ▶ If you add resources or change the network topology, you need to manually update the routes in your routing table.
    - ▶ Routers don't send "advertisements" to share info between networks.
    - ▶ You need to occasionally restart your **VPN tunnel** (p170).
    - ▶ All this can work well in small networks that don't change frequently.
- Cloud Router uses the **BGP** protocol for **dynamic routing** –

- ▶ You configure a **BGP session** so that the connected networks can automatically discover topology changes.
- ▶ An additional IP address has to be assigned to each end of the VPN tunnel.
- ▶ Cloud Router "advertises" subnets from its VPC and learns on-prem routes.
- ▶ This often adds new path options for traffic between the networks, and as a result, it can improve auto failover and load balancing across resources in these networks.
- ▶ This works also for large and complex networks.
- You need to use "custom" route advertisements if you want to also advertise external IPs or routes from a different network peered to yours.
- You can use Cloud Router and BGP, while at the same time also have static routes to specific GCP resources.
- For redundancy, you can create two VPN tunnels connecting the on-prem network to two GCP regions, with a Cloud Router in each GCP region.
- You can set up two different BGP sessions in order to maintain two parallel sets of routes in the same VPC – for example, to connect the test subnet in one session and the production subnet in another.
- Cloud Router can advertise either regional subnets only or all subnets in the network, depending on whether the VPC's **dynamic routing mode** is global or regional.
- Cloud Router creates **custom dynamic routes** to the various destinations of your network traffic. If there are multiple possible routes to the same destination, it needs to pick the best path. This can be done in different ways.
  - ▶ When the decision is made by a single Cloud Router, it uses the lowest **AS path length**. The AS path length is the number of "next hops" (p147) needed to reach a destination.
  - ▶ When the decision is made by multiple Cloud Routers, it uses the "base priority" measure instead of the AS path length. A key input into the "base priority" is the Multi-Exit Discriminator (**MED**).
  - ▶ MED is a priority attribute of on-prem routers, which you manually specify. You can use it, for example, to show that you prefer your Dedicated Interconnect (p173) over

VPN, or to keep a "backup" tunnel available. MED values are advertised by your on-prem router.

▶ The above is sufficient when using regional dynamic routing (p148), where you only select a route in the same region. When using global dynamic routing (p148), a route is selected for each region. The **route metric** for the global priority calculation still uses MED but it also includes a **regional cost** element. The regional cost is provided by Google and can't be modified.

▶ If routes have the same AS path lengths and same MED values, traffic is spread across all routes by using "equal cost multi path" (ECMP).

- Cloud Router settings include –
  ▶ "Keepalive time". This defines how often BGP info is exchanged between routers.
  ▶ "Hold timer". This indicates how long to wait before removing routes learned long ago.
  ▶ "Stale path timer". This defines how long a router will wait before deleting learned routes, after the other router doesn't let it use these routes.
  ▶ "Graceful restart". This defines how long a router would wait for the other one to restart before it concludes something is wrong. It's less important if you have redundant routers and tunnels.

8.11 Cloud VPN

A virtual private network (**VPN**) is an extension of a private network, so that it can be accessed by remote users over the internet. The remote users access the network as if they were local, despite the use of a public network to make the connection. The connection is called a **VPN tunnel**.

Cloud VPN is the GCP implementation, which securely connects your VPC to a peer network somewhere else. The peer network can be on-prem or in another cloud.
- Cloud VPN, like Cloud Interconnect (p172), can help you build hybrid solutions, partially in GCP and partially elsewhere.

Cloud VPN is the cheaper alternative since traffic between the networks doesn't use a private connection.

- The cloud VPN connection uses the IPsec protocol. It also uses the IKE protocol (internet key exchange) for authentication.
- Traffic travelling between the two networks is encrypted by a **VPN gateway** on one side and decrypted by a VPN gateway on the other side.
- The peer VPN gateway must have a static external IP address.
- Each Cloud VPN tunnel can support a network bandwidth of up to 3 Gbps.
- Cloud VPN attempts to detect "replay" attacks. "Replays" are malicious attempts to intervene with the data packets sent over the public network, by delaying or reusing them. The detection looks at the latest 4096 packets; if a packet arrives and it doesn't belong in this window, it is discarded.
- Cloud VPN can be used in VPCs or in legacy networks (p147).

GCP has two types of Cloud VPN gateways: high-availability VPN (HA) and Classic VPN. **HA VPN** lets you peer a network outside GCP to a VPC network in single region.

- HA VPN has built-in redundancy, so that it can offer a 99.99% availability. But note that availability on the peer side remains your responsibility.
- To establish a HA VPN, you need to create two VPN tunnels.
- GCP automatically assigns two public IPs to two **interfaces** on the HA VPN gateway in your VPC.
- There are three different ways you can set up these tunnels and interfaces:
  - ▶ Two VPN gateway devices in the peer network, with one tunnel from each of them to its own interface in the VPC.
  - ▶ One VPN gateway device in the peer network, with two interfaces. Each interface has its own tunnel to its own interface in the VPC.
  - ▶ One VPN gateway device in the peer network, with one interface. Each tunnel connects this interface to a separate interface in the VPC.
- All routing is dynamic and based on BGP (p168).
- You can use HA VPN to connect two different networks on GCP. You'll need HA gateways on both sides.

- You configure route priorities for HA VPN tunnels as either active/active or active/passive.
  - ▶ In an active/passive config, your peer gateway advertises the peer network's routes with different MED values (p169) for each tunnel. Your Cloud Router imports these as custom dynamic routes (p169) in your VPC, with different priorities, and also advertises ingress routes with different priorities for each tunnel. The route with the highest priority is used whenever possible, so by default only one tunnel is used.
  - ▶ In an active/active config, your peer gateway advertises the peer network's routes with the same MED values for each tunnel. Your Cloud Router imports these as custom dynamic routes in your VPC, with identical priorities, and also advertises ingress routes with equal priorities for each tunnel. Traffic in both directions uses both tunnels, and the connection can have their combined throughput.
  - ▶ You can assign MED values so that route priorities vary by the type of traffic. This allows routing configs that are more complex than active/active or active/passive.

Classic VPN is a name for any Cloud VPN gateway created before the introduction of HA VPN.
- Classic VPN gateways have a single interface and a single external IP address.
- Classic tunnels can use either dynamic (BGP) or static routing.
- Their SLA offers 99.9% availability. You need to create a public IP address and a forwarding rule.

8.12 Cloud Interconnect

Like Cloud VPN, **Cloud Interconnect** helps you build hybrid solutions, connecting networks in GCP and on-prem. Unlike Cloud VPN, Interconnect uses a private connection, and your data doesn't traverse the internet.
- Cloud Interconnect gives you lower latency than Cloud VPN but at a higher cost. You need to consider this tradeoff in the context of your own requirements.

172

- With Cloud Interconnect, private IPs in each network are directly accessible from the other. You don't need to set up NAT or VPN. But you need to ensure IP ranges don't overlap.
- Cloud Interconnect uses a "virtual LAN" (**VLAN**) approach to create a tunnel between networks. The Interconnect itself is the physical connection that goes all the way to your on-prem router. You add a VLAN **attachment** to a Cloud Router in your VPC, to link it to the Interconnect.
- A VLAN attachment supports one region and one VPC. But you can use multiple attachments with one Interconnect, to connect it to multiple VPCs or to different regions in one VPC.
- You decide the capacity of each attachment. A higher capacity costs more (amazingly).
- Your Cloud Router dynamically exchange routes with your on-prem router via a BGP session (p169).
- You can create a "hub and spoke" structure, linking multiple VPCs to your on-prem network, as long as you only include one on-prem network. Linking on-prem networks to each other using Cloud Interconnect violates the GCP terms.
- The connection between GCP and your on-prem network doesn't always have auto encryption; this depends on the specific GCP service you use over the Interconnect. You can add encryption at the app level, or set up your own VPN solution to use the Interconnect, but you can't use Cloud Interconnect and Cloud VPN together.
- There are two ways of setting up a Cloud Interconnect: either Dedicated Interconnect or Partner Interconnect.

Dedicated Interconnect (DI in short) is the Interconnect available in any of Google's metros (p15). Each metro supports some GCP regions.
- Your DI is made of one or multiple 10 Gbps circuits, or 100 Gbps circuits (one or two, so up to 200 Gbps).
- To use DI, you need to extend your on-prem network so that it reaches a Google colocation facility. Your on-prem router is located at this facility, and forms a "cross connect" to a **Google Peering Edge**.
- The Peering Edge is physically adjacent to your on-prem router but is within your GCP project. The Peering Edge connects to a Cloud Router in your VPC.

- The on-prem device you install in the colocation facility needs to meet some technical requirements from Google.
- You need to configure BGP (p168) on your on-prem routers and Cloud Routers.
- You configure DI with some redundancy. Google has two recommended setups, one for 99.99% availability and another for 99.9% availability.
- The following setting is needed to achieve 99.99% availability:
  - ▶ Four DIs, 2 + 2, in different metros. This means four different instances of an on-prem router connected to a Google Peering Edge.
  - ▶ Within each metro, each DI is in a different edge availability domain (p16), so 4 metro zones are involved (2 per metro). Each metro has at least two zones, which go down for maintenance at different times.
  - ▶ Four Cloud Routers, 2 + 2, in different GCP regions, even if your VMs are all in one region. There may be a partial match between regions and metros.
  - ▶ Each Cloud Router must be attached to a different DI, so you need 4 different VLAN attachments.
  - ▶ The dynamic routing mode for the VPC network must be "global", so that resources in one region can link to Cloud Routers in another region.
  - ▶ Your on-prem network can have either one router or two. If there are two, each one can connect to one GCP region.
- For non-critical apps, a setting that offers 99.9% availability may be sufficient. This setting is based on creating DI resources in one region only: two DIs in different edge availability domains, connected to two different Cloud Routers.

Partner Interconnect (PI in short) is an Interconnect offered not directly by Google but by their supported providers.
- You should consider using PI if you don't require the high bandwidth of DI, or if you can't physically extend your on-prem network to reach a colocation facility.
- Different providers offer their own PI locations. Each location supports a subset of GCP regions. The PI provider's location is connected to Google's network. You'll need to connect your on-prem network to the provider's network.

- PI providers offer a range of bandwidths, including some at lower capacities than DI, starting from 50 Mbps. These may be more suitable for your needs.
- Some providers offer what's known as **layer 2 connections** –
    - ▶ The traffic between your GCP and on-prem networks passes through the service provider's network, but it doesn't stop there.
    - ▶ You need to configure BGP (p168) directly between your on-prem router and the Cloud Router in your VPC.
    - ▶ To get 99.99% availability, 4 virtual circuits are needed, split between two metros, and also 4 BGP sessions, so that each Cloud Router is connected to an on-prem router.
- Some providers offer what's known as **layer 3 connections** –
    - ▶ Traffic is sent to a destination in the service provider's network, and then sent from there to its real destination in the on-prem or VPC network.
    - ▶ A Peering Edge in the service provider's network is responsible for the connection to your on-prem router.
    - ▶ BGP between the service provider and your VPC is automated.
    - ▶ BGP between the service provider and your on-prem router will usually be automated.
    - ▶ To get 99.99% availability, 4 circuits are needed between your VPC and your service provider, split between two metros, and also 4 BGP sessions, so that each Cloud Router is connected to a different Interconnect in the service provider's network.
- Your availability SLA only applies to connectivity between your VPC and the service provider's network; it isn't an end-to-end SLA since it excludes the link to your on-prem network.
- Similar to DI, if you create your PI resources in one region only, you can get 99.9% availability.

It's worth mentioning **Direct Peering** (DP in short), even though it isn't part of GCP and it doesn't require use of GCP.
- DP is linked to Google services outside GCP, such as G Suite.
- It's a direct, high-throughput path between your on-prem network and Google's private network, so it can be used to access your GCP resources.

- It's available at Google's network edge locations (p15).
- If you use DP for traffic from a VPC, it will be sent via either the default internet gateway (p147) or a Cloud VPN tunnel.
- DP doesn't use VLAN attachments. Your Cloud Routers don't learn router to your on-prem network.
- DP has no setup or maintenance costs, just traffic egress rates, which are lower than the Interconnect rates if the destination IP address is your on-prem network.
- To use DP, you need to meet Google's technical peering requirements. Your network needs to have a publicly routable Autonomous System Number (ASN); publicly routable address space; 24x7 network ops centre (NOC) capable of resolving BGP routing issues; presence at one of the Internet Exchanges (IXPs) or a listed private peering interconnection facility; a range of physical requirements (port types, subnet size, link types and others); and many other requirements.

Carrier Peering is similar to DP but provided by third-party partners.
- Similar to DP, it isn't part of GCP but can connect to your GCP resources, and offers lower egress rates.
- Similar to DP, traffic from a VPC will be sent via the default internet gateway or a Cloud VPN tunnel.
- You'd typically use it either if you need to transfer lower data volumes than you'd do with DP, or if you can't meet the DP technical requirements.

8.13 Cloud CDN

Content delivery networks (CDNs) are data centres, located around the world, where files or data in high demand are cached, so that users can access them quickly while reducing the load on the file provider's servers.

Cloud CDN is a CDN service in GCP. It works the HTTP(S) load balancing service (p160).
- The front end IPs and ports that receive requests from users, and the backends that respond to these requests, are all defined in the HTTP(S) load balancer.

- In the CDN context, these backends are sometimes called **origin servers**.
- User requests from an HTTP(S) load balancer arrive at the GFE (p157). The load balancer finds the relevant backend in the URL map. If this backend has a Cloud CDN, the GFE checks if the user's request already has a response cached in the CDN.
- If the GFE finds a cached response (**cache hit**), it sends it to the user (**cache egress**).
- If there's no cached response (**cache miss**), the GFE makes a request to the load balancer and waits for a response. The header of the response should indicate whether it is cacheable. If it is, the GFE stores it in the Cloud CDN (**cache fill**).
- Cache fill happens only in response to a client request. You can't fill the cache in advance.
- On a cache miss, the GFE might attempt to get the content from a nearby cache through "cache-to-cache fill".
- The cache has a capacity limit. If it's full, the CDN can still add content if it finds "unpopular" content that it can **evict**.
- Content also have an expiration time which you can specify. When content expires, it is removed from the cache.
- On "hits", you pay for cache egress traffic. On "misses", you also pay for cache fill. So "hits" are cheaper.
- The **hit ratio** is the percentage of requests that can be served from the cache. The ratio for each origin server is shown in the GCP console.
- You can remove items from the cache (i.e. "invalidate" them).
- You can view logs to see what gets served from the cache.
- Cloud Armor (p193) is not supported for Cloud CDN: you can't associate an Armor policy with a backend service with a CDN.

CDN Interconnect is a GCP service that allows you to serve data from your GCP project through a third-party CDN provider.
- Google allow some providers to peer with GCP network edge locations (p15), so that their CDNs can access your content.
- You'd consider this service if your egress volumes are high.
- Data sent to approved providers is charged at a reduced rate.

Chapter 9
Security services

9.1 Cloud IAM

No matter how you use GCP, there will always be things you must do to keep your cloud resources and data safe. You need to protect them from the bad guys out there, who wish you compromise the confidentiality, integrity or availability (p5) of your resources, and there might also be bad guys within your org with similar intentions.

Your journey to security in GCP starts with **Cloud IAM**, which is the framework for **identity and access management**. The way you use IAM should be consistent with the principle of "least privilege" (p79, p151).

- Almost everything you do across all GCP services involves an API call, either explicitly or behind the scenes. Every such API call is access-controlled with Cloud IAM.
- IAM permissions can be defined separately for each feature of each GCP service, so you can use Cloud IAM to specify "who can do what" in a lot of detail.
- Access to your GCP resources can be given to any **member**. A member can be any of the following:
    - ▶ The Google account of a user
    - ▶ A service account (p181)
    - ▶ A Google group with multiple users
    - ▶ A G Suite domain (p25)
    - ▶ A Cloud Identity domain (p183)
- A member is always represented by a unique email address, even if they're not a specific person (as in a Google group).
- You assign **permissions** to members, but you shouldn't do it directly. Directly giving permissions to specific members isn't a scalable practice: if you manage many members, you'll have so much work, that sooner or later some members will have the wrong permissions. This could easily happen when a user moves to a different team or leaves the org.
- Here's what you do instead:

- ▶ Assign permissions to **roles**
- ▶ Create **groups** that contain all users that do a similar job
- ▶ Create **IAM policies** that **bind** groups to roles

- This practice of using groups and roles to assign permissions is safer, because most of the work is done in advance by creating roles, groups and policy bindings. When an individual joins, leaves or moves, you don't need to change any roles – you just add or remove this person in the relevant groups.
- Typical groups include org admins, network admins, security policy admins, billing admins, ops, developers. You can create other groups with different responsibilities.
- Each GCP service has its own built-in list of permissions, based on the actions that can be performed in this service. They have the structure "service.resource.action", for example "storage.buckets.delete". These permissions can get very specific, e.g. "storage.hmacKeys.get".
- Quite often, in order to complete what looks like one operation, you actually need multiple permissions. For example, to use the transfer service into BigQuery, you need "bigquery.transfers.update" and "bigquery.datasets.update".
- Permissions can be assigned to roles in different ways:
  - ▶ **Primitive roles**. A member can be the "owner", "editor" or "viewer" of a resource, and a set of permissions comes with each one of these options. An "owner" role can only be granted in the GCP Console. These roles are a crude way of giving permissions, and it's better to avoid them. They're still used for consistency with older versions.
  - ▶ **Predefined roles**. Each GCP service has its own set of built-in roles. Each role has its own preset group of permissions. In many cases using these existing roles will suit your needs.
  - ▶ **Custom roles**. If a predefined role doesn't have the set of permissions you want to give to members, you can group permissions in any way you like in a custom role.
- To see which permissions are included in which role, you can use the gcloud "describe" option or the roles.get() API.
- Once you've defined the roles you need, you should create **IAM policies** for your GCP resources. A policy is a file (JSON or YAML) that defines **bindings** between roles, members and

conditions: a specified role will be assigned to the specified members if the condition is met.
- The conditions in your IAM policy can restrict access to your resources based on attributes of the access request. Request details that can be used in these conditions include the date, time, URL hostname, URL path, or the destination IP address and port.
- Each policy also includes an audit config field (to decide what info gets logged); a version field (to let you store multiple versions of a policy and easily identify the latest); and an "etag" field (which helps if you use the same policy across systems – you should check the value of this field to verify it hasn't changed since the last check).
- The way you use Cloud IAM is linked to the way you organise your GCP resources in a hierarchy of orgs, folders, projects (p21) and other resources. There are various parent-child relationships in this hierarchy, and you can set a Cloud IAM policy at any level in the resource hierarchy.
- Resources inherit the policies of their parent. The effective policy for a resource is the union of the policies you define for the resource itself and for its parents. So, for example, a GAE instance will inherit the policies of the project it's in, and the project will inherit the policies of the folder and org they're in.
- This inheritance only works in one direction. So, for example, if you define an IAM policy for a Pub/Sub topic (p47), this policy will not apply to any other resource. To ensure you attach the right permissions to each resource, you need to attach them at a suitable level of the org hierarchy.
- If this doesn't work well then maybe you should change the resource hierarchy. For example, if two resources don't need to share any IAM policy, then it may be better to put them in separate projects.
- Calls to the IAM policy API, and changes that influence permissions (such as the membership of Google groups), should be logged and monitored. This kind of audit may be needed for compliance with regulatory frameworks, and should be considered essential even if not formally required.

A **service account** is a type of account that doesn't represent a human user, but still needs access to GCP APIs. If, for example, an app needs to write files to GCS (p73), it will need a service account to have access to the GCS API.

- Service accounts, like user accounts, are created using Cloud IAM, and you assign roles to them which give them specific permissions.
- If you have a long-running job to execute, you should run it under the identity and credentials of a service account, and not let the process "impersonate" a user.
- "Impersonation" is encouraged when it works in the other direction: a user can log in with the identity of a service account when they need short-term access to resources they usually don't use. You arrange for the service account to have access to the relevant API using an OpenID Connect JSON Web Token (**JWT**). The advantage of JWTs is that they are designed for short-term, time-limited access.
- Every service account has a **key pair**, i.e. a combination of a private key and private key, generated and implemented based on the RSA methodology. Your key pair can be either **GCP-managed** or **user-managed**. GCP-managed keys are used entirely within GCP; they cannot be downloaded, and they can be revoked when no longer needed. With user-managed ones, you need your own process for protecting, storing, revoking and recovering your keys.
- You should implement regular and automated **key rotation** using the IAM service account API. "Rotating" means periodically replacing the secret part of your access credentials, in order to minimise the impact in case someone gets access to this secret. Rotation is your responsibility with user-managed key pairs. With GCP-managed pairs this is handled automatically.
- Generally you should restrict who can log in with the identity of a service account, and limit the permissions of your service accounts to the minimum necessary.
- You should continuously monitor and audit the use of service accounts and their keys.

The **Cloud IAM recommender** helps you enforce the principle of "**least privilege**" by checking if the permissions you give to your members (p178) are really needed.
- It checks permissions and their usage by each user over the last 90 days.
- It highlights unused roles that can be revoked and under-utilised roles that can be replaced with a downgraded role.
- The recommender is not suitable for permissions used less often than every 90 days.

9.2 Other identity and access services

With Cloud IAM you can manage roles and use them to grant permissions to groups of users, but you can't use Cloud IAM to manage the user list itself. Your list of users is often managed via a specialised **directory** service, where you keep a profile for every user, with personal attributes that other services can query based on their specific needs. A connection between a directory service and the apps that need it is sometimes based on the common **LDAP** protocol.

The following are some common ways to manage your list of users in GCP:
- Just add users as needed when specifying roles and permissions, with no further management. This can only work well in a very simple org.
- Use Google's G Suite (p32) as your user directory.
- Use **Cloud Identity** (p183) as a stand-alone service for managing users. Note that Cloud Identity isn't the same as Identity Platform (p185). I suspect Google might keep renaming these services, which can cause confusion because of their similar titles, so look out for updates from Google.
- Use the popular **Microsoft Activity Directory** (**AD**), installed in your on-prem data centre, and sync it with GCP using the LDAP-compliant Google Cloud Directory Sync, GCDS (p184).
- Installed Microsoft AD on GCP using Managed AD (p184).

Cloud Identity provides "Identity as a Service (IDaaS)". It's not part of GCP, but you can use it as the directory of your GCP users.

- Relying on Cloud Identity as your user directory is most sensible if your org users a range of Google products, and not just GCP, since it easily integrates with these.
- The idea of IDaaS is that everything to do with creating, querying and managing users and groups is handled via a set of API endpoints. You can use these endpoints to administer your users in any way you want, in GCP or elsewhere.
- You use Cloud Identity for user authentication (p5) and you can set up various capabilities related to authentication:
  - ▶ **Single sign-on** (**SSO**) – the ability to use the same identity to log into different services.
  - ▶ **Multi-factor authentication** (**MFA**) – a requirement to authenticate in multiple stages, for example using a password followed by a verification code sent to a personal device.
  - ▶ **Two-step verification** (**2SV**) – another name for the common MFA approach described above.
  - ▶ Authentication parameter config, such as session length, password strength, self-service password recovery.
- Cloud Identity can also be used as your "enterprise mobility management" (EMM) product. This means you can use it to record all devices available to your users and manage these devices through passcode management, device search, map devices to users, screen locks and so on.
- It has a free edition and a premium one. The premium edition offers more automation features, although the free version is sufficient in many business scenarios.
- You can use Cloud Identity to create a "node" that links between an org (p21), a domain (p25), a list of GCP projects and billing accounts (p25).

Google's recommended **two-step verification** (2SV or MFA) approach is based on the FIDO standard.
- It requires users to hold a physical device, either a "Titan key" or their Android phone.
- The additional step in their authentication sequence is simple, and only involves clicking a button.

- This performs a dual verification: it makes sure users are logging into the service they originally registered a security key with, and it ensures that the correct security key is used.

If you like what Cloud Identity offers bur your main directory is kept somewhere else, you can keep them both in sync using **Google Cloud Directory Sync, GCDS**.
- This is a form of **identity federation**: it lets you control how users that authenticate elsewhere (with a third-party or on-prem directory) access your GCP resources.
- GCDS can be used to let GCP access your Microsoft AD (p182) users, groups, shared contacts, user profiles, calendar resources, and any other info stored on an LDAP server.
- You set up **rules** to specify what exactly gets synced. You will need to register a scheduled task to run the sync process continuously.
- The sync is strictly one-way: data is only updated at the Google end, never on the side of the directory provider.
- Although often used with Microsoft AD, you can run GCDS on either Windows or Linux.
- When connecting on-prem Microsoft AD infrastructure to GCP, you can run GCDS either on-prem or in a VM on GCE (p33). Installing GCDS on-prem is preferred because the link to AD might be unencrypted, whereas the link between GCDS and Cloud Identity is encrypted with HTTPS.
- GCDS includes a UI tool called "Configuration Manager".
- A **domain controller** (**DC**) is a name for a Microsoft AD server. When connecting GCDS to an org with multiple DC instances, it's best to use the "DC Locator" mechanism of AD to choose dynamically which DC to connect to.

An alternative to GCDS is Google's **Managed Microsoft AD**: a managed, real Microsoft AD domain controller, running in GCP.
- Using this service means that your user directory follows the Microsoft approach but resides inside your VPC (p144) on GCP.
- This service runs DCs on Windows VMs on GCP. It maintains these servers for you and ensures their high availability.

- If you choose Managed Microsoft AD, Google recommend that you deploy it in all regions where you have GCP resources that you'd like to authenticate to using AD. In every region you choose, it will run DCs in at least two zones.
- In the Microsoft AD language, things like users, groups and computers are all **objects** in your directory. In the Managed AD service, when you create a **domain**, it automatically creates some objects adjusted for work on GCP:
    ▶ A "cloud" org unit (OU) to host the objects you manage.
    ▶ A "cloud service objects" OU for objects managed by AD.
    ▶ Several groups within the "cloud service objects" OU, for users with different roles.
    ▶ Group policy objects (GPOs), including a default computer policy, to apply some config settings to multiple users.
    ▶ Several users, including a "setup admin" (for you) and a "cloud service admin" (a service account for AD to use).
- You can opt in for options such as server patching, health monitoring and automated backups.
- You decide which VPCs can use your AD domain. You can then use AD in these VPCs and also in any other env (including on-prem or other clouds) that connects to these VPCs using VPN or Cloud Interconnect (p172).

The services we've just reviewed help you create and manage your list of users. A separate question is how users will sign into your apps. The **Identity Platform** can help with this.

- Users that authenticate using Identity Platform have a fixed set of basic properties: ID, primary email address, name, photo URL. If you choose to add other user properties, you store them in your own database.
- You can use Identity Platform to set up authentication using any of the following methods -
    ▶ Using email and password
    ▶ By phone with SMS verification
    ▶ Using identity federation (p184) with the user's Google, Facebook, Twitter or GitHub account
    ▶ Using identity federation with any custom system that can exchange access tokens based on the OAuth2 / OpenID Connect (p9) or SAML methodologies
    ▶ Allowing login as an anonymous user.

- You can use the Identity Platform SDK to build these options into your own web and mobile solutions.
- You can associate more than one sign-in method with a user.
- The confirmation that a user is signed in is passed as a signed JWT (p9, p181) which you can send to a backend server. You can use custom JWTs and your own process of signing them, if you want different user info to be passed to the backend.
- If a user is currently signed in using Identity Platform, this is reflected in the **state** of an **Auth instance**. You can track any changes to the state of an Auth instance using "listeners".
- Identity Platform features are also available via **Cloud Identity for Customers and Partners** (**CICP**) or **Firebase Authentication**.
   - ▶ Google offer these, confusingly, as separate products.
   - ▶ They provide similar features as Identity Platform, but the target audience is providers of apps on Firebase (p30) or anyone adding a GCP backend to a non-GCP service.
   - ▶ An additional feature of Firebase authentication is its own **security rules** concept, that work with GCS, Firestore and Realtime Database. In each rule you define a path to specific data and conditions that must be met to allow access to that path.

Cloud Identity-Aware Proxy (IAP) is a security mechanism at the app level. It can help you control access to solutions you build in GCP if they are accessed using HTTPS.

- When an app or a resource are protected by Cloud IAP, they can only be accessed by users with the right IAM roles (p179).
- When GAE or the HTTPS Load Balancer receive a request, they check if IAP is enabled. If it's enabled then they check the user's sign-in status, IAM role and permissions. Access to the protected app depends on having suitable permissions.
- You can use IAP with HTTPS services you run on GCE (p33) and GKE (p52), but note that IAP doesn't provide full protection in cases where a user has access to the same VM, cluster or project where your app is. Such access might allow these users to bypass the IAP authentication.

- HTTP requests you send to your IAP should have **signed headers** using JWTs. This means that you include in your request some info, encrypted with the ES256 algorithm, which can be used for user authorisation (p5). The "kid" JWT header should include your IAP public key, and the JWT itself should be signed using the corresponding private key.
- When you test your implementation of IAP, you can visit your app using a special "secure_token_test" URL, provided by IAP, which will deliberately pass an invalid JWT to your app. There are other **special URLs** available for various test scenarios.

9.3 Data Loss Prevention

Cloud Data Loss Prevention (**DLP**) is a data scanning service, which can help you identify, classify and redact sensitive info in the data. Common types of sensitive data include credit card numbers, names, phone numbers and credentials.

- DLP can work with data already stored on GCP (e.g. in GCS, BigQuery or Datastore) or data from external sources.
- It has built-in **detectors** to identify patterns and formats of sensitive data. The detectors can consider the context and not just the data item itself.
- You can add custom detectors by creating dictionaries, regular expressions or rules that specify what info is sensitive.
- You create a DLP job **trigger** (e.g. run the job daily) and define an **action** to perform once the job is done. The action can be either saving the DLP scan results to BigQuery or publishing them to a Pub/Sub channel.
- The title of this service can be misleading; DLP doesn't directly prevent the loss of data. The main features of DLP include –
  - ▶ **Classifying** an incoming text stream by sensitivity. The output of a DLP scan is a list of findings with the info type of each record, likelihood (i.e. confidence in the identified type) and offset (i.e. where the info is in the data).
  - ▶ Classifying **text in images**. It uses Optical Character Recognition (OCR) to recognise text prior to classification. The outputs show a "bounding box" where text was found.
  - ▶ **Redacting** text that belongs to certain classes. Redacting data can be done by **masking**, **hashing**, **tokenising**, **format-preserving encryption** and other techniques.

- ▶ Generalising data by **bucketing**. An example of bucketing would be to convert specific dates to longer periods, so that each data point becomes less specific.
- ▶ Identifying dates and performing **shifting**, i.e. changing them randomly while preserving the sequence and duration. Usually the dates of each individual are shifted by a fixed amount of time, unique to that individual.
- ▶ **Pseudo-anonymisation** or **tokenisation**, i.e. replacing sensitive data with substitutes in a consistent way. You retain a known mapping between records before and after the tokenisation, so if needed, you may be able to reverse the de-identified values back to the original ones.
- DLP offers several metrics to quantify the risk that a de-identified dataset can be re-identified. These metrics include:
  - ▶ "K-anonymity": a dataset is k-anonymous if a set of partially-identifying attributes of each person is identical to at least k−1 other people.
  - ▶ "L-diversity": an extension of k-anonymity, that also measures the diversity of values for each attribute.
  - ▶ "K-map": similar to the two above, but for small datasets.
  - ▶ "Delta-presence": a method to estimate the probability that a given user in a larger population is present in the dataset. This is useful in cases where membership of the dataset is itself considered sensitive info.
- All these stats can be used when deciding on the tradeoff between privacy protection and your analytical needs.

9.4 Managing keys and secrets

Cloud key management service (KMS) lets you generate, use, rotate, and destroy cryptographic keys. It can also create digital signatures.
- It can generate crypto keys with various algorithms: AES256, RSA 2048, RSA 3072, RSA 4096, EC P256, EC P384.
- Your KMS keys can be used for any of the following:
  - ▶ **Symmetric encryption**, i.e. encryption via a symmetric process, so that the same key can also be used for decryption.

- ▶ **Asymmetric encryption**, i.e. encryption using a public key, so that only the holder of a matching private key (from the same **key pair**) can decrypt the data.
- ▶ **Digital signature**, i.e. signing info with a private key, so that others can use the matching public key (from the same **key pair**) to verify the info is authentic.
- Cloud KMS resources have resource IDs like any other GCP resource. KMS resources are stored in a hierarchical structure: **org > project > location > key ring > key > key version**.
- A key ring is a group of keys, all stored in one location and associated with one project. You put different keys in the same ring if you want them to have similar permissions. Operations such as revoking permissions can be done at the key ring level.
- Keys are not stored at the org level, but the policies (p24) that define their permissions can be inherited from the relevant org. You can run KMS in a separate project if you don't want the project owner to also own the keys; the admin at the org level can set policies to restrict access to keys.
- The location of your keys can be one of the following:
  - ▶ Regional keys
  - ▶ Dual-regional keys, stored in two GCP regions you select (can be used with GCS only)
  - ▶ Multi-regional keys, stored in more than two regions
  - ▶ Global keys, stored in all GCP regions
- The **key material** is the actual set of bits used for encryption, i.e. the key itself. It is used for encryption and decryption, but the key material can never be viewed or exported from KMS.
- The key material can change over time if you create new versions of the same key. A **key version** includes the key material at a specific point in time.
- A **symmetric key** at any point in time will have a primary key version. Creating a new primary version will rotate the symmetric key, but you won't lose access to past versions.
- **Asymmetric keys** are more complex because they come in pairs, and the user may share the public portion of the pair with others. For this reason, asymmetric keys don't have a primary version, and key rotation is not automated.

189

- Files encrypted with the same key may be encrypted with different versions of it. When you ask KMS to decrypt any one of these files, you don't need to specify the version – this will be identified automatically.
- Keys, key rings and key versions can't be deleted, but you can destroy the key material. The possible **states** of a key version are: enabled, disabled, scheduled for destruction, or destroyed.
- The key material has a type, indicating the length of the key and the algorithm which will be used with it. KMS uses probabilistic encryption: encrypting the same data twice with the same key version will not produce the same ciphertext.
- KMS integrates with Cloud IAM (p178) and Audit Logs (p209), so that you can manage key permissions, monitor how keys are used, and monitor admin activity.
- In terms of their function in your solution, you can work with different types of keys - DEKs, KEKs, CMEKs and CSEKs:
  - ▶ Your data is encrypted with a **data encryption key** (**DEK**). You don't have to use KMS for generating the DEK or for encrypting your data. You can store the DEK somewhere near the data it encrypts. You replace the DEK every time you write data, so you don't need to rotate it.
  - ▶ The DEK is encrypted with a **key encryption key** (**KEK**). The idea of encrypting the encryption key is called "envelope encryption". You decide which DEKs you encrypt with the same KEK. You never store the KEK near the DEK. The KEK is generated and stored in KMS, and never leaves KMS. You rotate the KEK regularly.
  - ▶ You may prefer a **customer-managed encryption key** (**CMEK**). CMEK is a specific type of KEK. You still use a DEK and a KEK, and you still use KMS to create and store your KEK in a key ring. The main difference is that you have more control over the way the CMEK is used in different actions you perform on your data.
  - ▶ In GCS and GCE you can use a **customer-supplied encryption key** (**CSEK**). This option is similar to CMEK but it takes your own control one step further, by letting you supply a KEK that you have generated.

- Because symmetric encryption is a more efficient process than asymmetric encryption, most encryption is done symmetrically. The main info encrypted asymmetrically is the symmetric encryption key itself, when following the envelope encryption approach.
  - ▶ Asymmetric encryption (KEK) of the symmetric encryption key (DEK) provides a good balance between encryption performance and confidentiality.
  - ▶ Anyone with access to the symmetric DEK can encrypt and decrypt the data.
  - ▶ Anyone with access to the public part of the KEK can encrypt the DEK.
  - ▶ Only KMS can then decrypt the DEK using the private part of the KEK.
- KMS is implemented by software, but it can integrate with **Cloud HSM** – a separate service that offers hardware-based protection of your keys.
  - ▶ Cloud HSM is a managed cloud-hosted **hardware security module** (HSM) service. The hardware used is FIPS 140-2 Level 3 certified HSMs.
  - ▶ You can use it to encrypt, decrypt, and sign data.
  - ▶ It can use AES-256 symmetric and RSA 2048, RSA 3072, RSA 4096, EC P256, EC P384 asymmetric crypto keys.
  - ▶ You can verify that a key was created in the HSM with **attestation tokens**.

While KMS storage focuses entirely on crypto keys, **Secret Manager** is a service you can use to store other types of secrets.
- Secret Manager is a good place to store passwords, access keys and certificates that need retrieving while apps runs.
- A secret can be a text string or any other binary object.
- Unlike keys in KMS, where you can never see or export the key material, a secret can be viewed if you have the right permissions.
- The secrets you store have versions, similar to key versions in KMS. They can also have custom metadata, which you can use for filtering secrets for different needs.

9.5 Protection from threats

This section reviews several GCP services that can add more layers of defense to your solution. Some of these protect you by providing additional tools for restricting and monitoring access. Others introduce more specialised defense mechanisms, that focus on specific types of security threat.

VPC Service Controls (**VPCSC**) allow you to define a security boundary (or "perimeter") around GCP resources, to control the movement of data across this boundary.

- When you define a VPCSC perimeter, resources inside it can only be accessed privately. Access is allowed from clients in authorised networks, either in GCP or on-prem, using Private Google Access (p166).
- This mechanism is independent of Cloud IAM. Ideally you should use both. VPCSC will limit what can be done with your data even if an unauthorised user has somehow managed to access it – for example, in case of an "insider attack".
- Data can't be copied to unauthorised resources outside the perimeter (for example using *gsutil cp*).
- Resources within a perimeter don't have access to unauthorised (potentially public) resources outside the perimeter.
- You should still use other mechanisms to restrict access to metadata, since VPCSC doesn't cover this.
- Access requests from the internet to resources inside a perimeter are denied by default. You can change this by defining different request **access levels**. Access levels are defined by attributes such as the source IP address, client device or location. Access levels are specified using by the **Access Context Manager** service.
- A **perimeter bridge** allows projects in different security perimeters to access each other in a two-way link.

A "denial of service" attack (DoS) is when someone tries to make your systems unavailable by sending to them more requests than

192

they can handle. A "distributed DoS" (DDoS) is a special case where the attacker is sophisticated enough to send the requests from multiple sources, so that you can't simply block one source.

Cloud Armor is a service providing protection from DoS attacks. It works with your HTTP(S) load balancer (p160), since the load balancer is the most likely target of a DoS attack.

- Your define **security policies** for your backend services. One policy can be used by multiple backend services.
- The policy is made of "allow list" rules and "deny list" rules for specific IP address ranges (IPv4 or IPv6). Typically you'd only allow access to users from your org, and specific external partners.
- The "allow" and "deny" rules are implemented at Google's global edge locations. These rules are similar to firewall rules, except that Cloud Armor rules act on client traffic before it gets load balanced.
- You can configure a "deny" rule to display a 403, 404, or 502 error code.
- When you configure multiple rules, you can define the order in which the rules are evaluated.
- Cloud Armor activity is included in the load balancer log.
- The **preview mode** lets you see the potential effects of the rules in Cloud Logging without enforcing the rules.
- Each policy has a **fingerprint** field. The fingerprint is a hash of the contents of the policy. To update the policy, you need to provide the current fingerprint. This is a way of ensuring that policy updates are made by an authorised user.
- Cloud Armor rules don't filter traffic by IAM role. For this you'd use Identity-Aware Proxy (p186).
- Deny and allow lists are not supported for Cloud CDN or GCS.
- The "custom rules language" allows you to further customise your deny and allow rules and create an advanced filtering approach. You can define your rules based on the request method, headers, path, and other attributes. There are predefined rules for protection from other forms of attack, such as XSS (cross-site scripting) and SQL injection.

A **Shielded VM** is a GCE instance with verifiable integrity (p5).

- You use a Shielded VM to be confident that the boot process and the kernel code of your operating system haven't been compromised by malware.
- Protecting your operating system is an important step in preventing **data exfiltration**. Exfiltration is when someone makes unauthorised use of your data. Some attackers attempt to install "rootkits" on your operating system, which would allow them to bypass your access control mechanism.
- Shielded VMs go through a **secure boot**, verifying the digital signature of boot components using Google's Certificate Authority and Unified Extensible Firmware Interface (UEFI) firmware.
- In addition, **measured boot** is used, with the help of a virtual trusted platform module (vTPM). This module creates a known good boot baseline ("integrity policy baseline") and compares subsequent boots to it.
- Shielded VMs also run **integrity monitoring**, comparing platform configuration register (PCR) measurements between the most recent boot and the integrity policy baseline ("early boot" vs "late boot"), to highlight suspicious changes. You can modify the baseline if you want to indicate that some changes are legitimate. You can view integrity reports in Cloud Monitoring (p211), and set alerts on integrity failures.

Event Threat Detection is a service that scans your logs, looking for suspicious activity in your GCP envs.

- It has built-in rules that may help you detect all the following: malware, crypto-mining, unauthorised access, outgoing DDoS attacks, port scanning, and brute-force SSH.
- It can scan VPC flow logs (p146), Audit Logs (p209), SSH logs and firewall logs.

Web Security Scanner is a service that draws your attention to security vulnerabilities in your GAE apps, GCE and GKE.

- The scanner "crawls" your app, follows URLs it finds, tries to enter various user inputs, triggers event handlers, pushes buttons, and clicks links.
- Using the scanner is like putting your cat on the keyboard; it can do risky things. You should scope the scan so that you don't let it perform undesirable actions.
- The scanner suggests where your solution might be vulnerable to attacks like XSS (cross-site scripting) and flash injection. It highlights risks such as mixed HTTP/HTTPS content, passwords in clear text, and use of unsafe Javascript libraries.

Cloud Security Command Centre (**SCC**) is a SIEM tool offered to GCP users. SIEM tools perform **security info and event management** by aggregating log data, analysing security alerts, authorising config changes, controlling access, and other things.

- SCC is a dashboard that gives you integrated access to other GCP security and resource management services: DLP (p187), Security Scanner (p194), Event Threat Detection (p194), Audit Logs (p209), and other services that have a role in threat management. You can use the SCC API to integrate these in your own security systems and workflows.
- **Cloud Anomaly Detection** is a feature which can warn you if it finds evidence of suspicious activity (indicating, for example, possible leakage of credentials) or of improper use of your VMs (e.g. for phishing, intrusion into other systems, or crypto-mining).
- **Binary Authorisation** is a feature that checks that only approved versions of container images are deployed on GKE.
- **Enterprise Phishing Protection** looks for suspicious URLs and reports them to Google's "safe browsing service" (which shows warnings when users access dangerous sites or files). It publishes phishing results in the SCC dashboard.
- **Cloud Security Health Analytics** is a SCC feature that presents general "findings" about the security state of your VMs, network and storage. For example, it may let you know about GCS buckets with public access, open firewall ports, stale encryption keys, or de-activated security logging.
- You can bring third-party security products or their findings into SCC. It can integrate with Acalvio, Capsule8, Cavirin, Chef, Check Point CloudGuard Dome9, Cloudflare, CloudQuest,

195

McAfee, Qualys, Redblaze, Redlock by Palo Alto Networks, StackRox, Tenable.io, Twistlock, and Forseti.
- You can export SCC data to Splunk or other SIEM tools for further analysis. It can send alerts using Cloud Pub/Sub.
- SCC uses security marks (p22) to label your resources.

Forseti Security is a collection of open-source, community-driven tools to secure GCP solutions. It is made of several independent modules, which you can run on GCE or GKE.

- "**Inventory**" creates a snapshot of the inventory of your GCP resources, so you have a historical record of your architecture. The inventory is needed before running other Forseti services.
- "**Scanner**" audits your role-based access policies and ACLs based on a set of JSON or YAML rules you specify.
- "**Enforcer**" lets you define the desired state of your GCE firewall policies, and then compare the current and desired states. If there are differences, Enforcer can make changes using GCP APIs.
- "**Explain**" adds clarity to Cloud IAM policies by showing you explicitly what their impact is. It can show who has what access to which resources, which policy is the reason why a specific permission was given, and what options you have if you want to grant a specific permission to a specific member. You can use it to list the resources accessible by a specific member or the members with access to a specific resource.

Table 12 contains a summary of services that have a role in protecting your GCP resources.

Table 12: protecting your GCP resources

GCP service	What does it help you protect?
Service accounts	Access from one internal service to another.
Cloud IAM	Access by members of your org to any GCP resource.
Identity-aware proxy	Access by members of your org to resources at the app (HTTPS) level.
GCDS, Managed AD	Access to any resource by members of your org who are listed in an external directory.
Cloud Identity	Your user directory and the authentication process.
2SV	Integrity of the sign-in process.
Identity Platform, CICP	The sign-in process.
DLP	Sensitive info within your data.
DEKs	Data stored anywhere in GCP.
KMS	The DEKs you use to encrypt data.
Secret Manager	Passwords, access keys, certificates.
VPCSC	Data movement across boundaries you define.
Cloud Armor	Load-balanced services, when they are under a DoS attack.
Event Threat Detection	Resources that you keep logs for.
Security Scanner	Apps running in GAE, GCE or GKE.
Cloud Anomaly Detection	GCE instances and some project-level activity.
Enterprise Phishing	Any resource that might be exposed to a malicious URL.
SCC, Security Health Analytics	Any resource (presenting findings from other services).

GCP service	What does it help you protect?
Forseti Security	Any resource affected by IAM policies.
Shielded VM	Integrity of GCE instances.
Security rules	Data access by Firebase users.
Shielded Nodes	Integrity of GKE cluster nodes.
Binary Authorisation	Integrity of containers.
GKE Sandbox	Isolation of containers.
Container Analysis	Container images.
ACLs	Access to GCS buckets and objects.
Signed URLs	Access to GCS objects.
Policy documents	Uploading to GCS buckets.
Retention policies, holds	Deletion and overwriting of GCS objects.
Bucket locks	Your GCS retention policies.
Integrity checking	Integrity of data transferred to/from GCS.
Hadoop Secure Mode	Authentication in multi-tenant Dataproc clusters.
IOT Core	Authentication of IoT devices.
VPC flow logs	The ability to monitor and analyse network traffic.
Routing table	Network traffic to and from your GCP resources.
Firewall	Network traffic to and from your GCP resources.
Other logs	The ability to monitor and analyse the access to your GCP resources and the way they are used.

Security   Compute   Container   Storage   Data services   Networking   Ops

9.6 Regulatory compliance

Your cloud architecture needs to meet the security standards that you set for your own org, but it often needs to also comply with regulations or legal standards that apply in your area of work. Some regulatory frameworks apply widely while others are only relevant in a specific niche. If you have customers in different countries and different industry sectors, you may be expected to comply with multiple frameworks at the same time.

There's one key thing to note about any framework you need to comply with: GCP usually makes it possible for you to be compliant, but just because you use GCP doesn't mean you're ok. Whether or not you meet regulatory requirements depends on your solution architectures, your data architectures, your policies and practices, so it remains your own responsibility, not Google's.

- **PCI DSS** is the Data Security Standard of the Payment Card Industry. It applies to orgs that handle credit card data.
    - ▶ The PCI DSS defines requirements and best practices for firewall config, password management, encryption, malware protection, access control, patch management, and many other topics.
    - ▶ It includes best practices for any env that stores or transfers cardholder data (**CDE**, cardholder data env). The cardholder has a **PAN** (primary account number) and other data.
    - ▶ The required practices often involve **tokenisation** (p188). The PAN should be unreadable anywhere it is stored.
    - ▶ Your PCI DSS compliance requirements depend on your "level", i.e. how many transactions the company performs. Level 1 is the highest, with over 6 million transactions per year.
    - ▶ Level 1 requires audits by a qualified security assessor (**QSA**) in addition to a self-assessment questionnaire (**SAQ**). Other levels can be validated via the SAQ.
    - ▶ GCP can support all levels, including level 1 providers.
    - ▶ PCI DSS compliance depends on the "SAQ Type", i.e. how the company handles payment card transactions. For

online payment processing, three types are the most important: A, A-EP and D.
- ▶ **Type A** covers **fully outsourced** payment processing. The payment could be made on the merchant's app in a frame that is operated by a payment processor, or on a separate app. The merchant only gets confirmation of payment without ever touching customer card data.
- ▶ **Type A-EP** covers cases where payment processing is outsourced, but the merchant has access to the customer card data (e.g. if card details are entered in a form in their app).
- ▶ **Type D** is when the **merchant is also the payment processor**. The requirements from backend servers and databases are most stringent in this type.
- ▶ GCP services and resources you may need to configure for PCI DSS compliance include service accounts, firewalls, VPCSC, Cloud VPN, Load Balancing, Cloud NAT, Cloud IAM, DLP, KMS, Cloud Logging and Monitoring, and others.

- **GDPR** is the data protection regulation of the European Union (EU). It adopts a wide definition of **personal data** that requires protection.
  - ▶ Personal data in GDPR includes any info that can be attributed to a person. This covers not only personal details, but also social media posts, photos, lifestyle preferences, transaction histories, IP addresses.
  - ▶ GDPR defines several key entities with different responsibilities. **Data subjects** are EU citizens and residents that you may hold data about. **Data controllers** can be anyone (like companies, traders or campaigners) who makes decisions about personal data. **Data processors** are those who access the data, usually based on instructions from the data controllers.
  - ▶ GDPR requires risk assessment of data storage and access; identifying personal data continuously; explicit consent by each individual; giving individuals the right to view their data and get a copy; giving them the right to remove their data or correct errors; and the right to refuse automated decision making based on the data.

- ▶ GDPR defines legitimate reasons to process personal data for marketing, and includes restrictions on data retention.
- ▶ For personal data that is retained for legitimate reasons, GDPR includes guidance for **pseudo-anonymisation** (p188) via encryption or tokenisation.

- Federal USA law refers to **PII** (Personally Identifiable Info).
  - ▶ PII includes any info that can be used, on its own or with other info, to distinguish one individual from another, locate or contact them. This includes info that can be used to re-identify anonymous data.
  - ▶ Not all GDPR personal data is PII, but every PII counts as personal data, since the EU definition is broader, so the EU law is stricter.

- **HIPAA** is the American law that protects the privacy and security of protected health information (**PHI**).
  - ▶ To retain HIPAA compliance with GCP you should review Google's Business Associate Agreement (**BAA**), which explains which GCP services meet HIPAA requirements.
  - ▶ The BAA cover the GCP infrastructure in all regions, but not all GCP services and features are certified.

- **SOX** is the common name of the Sarbanes-Oxley act, the USA law that protects shareholders and the general public from accounting errors and fraud in public companies.
  - ▶ SOX defines which business records must be archived and the number of years they should be kept for.
  - ▶ SOX may have an impact on your choice of what info to log and how to manage your logs.
  - ▶ You might want to consider SOX requirements when you plan what data (logs and other datasets) you archive in different storage classes (e.g. in BigQuery and GCS) and what retention policy (p71, p78) is right for your data.

- **ISO 27000** is a family of standards for info security management systems (ISMS), published jointly by the International Org for Standardisation (ISO) and the International Electrotechnical Commission (IEC).
  - ▶ ISO 27001 lists auditing and accreditation requirements.
  - ▶ ISO 27002 has more technical implementation guidance.

- ▶ GCP is certified as ISO 27001 compliant. There's a list of GCP services with the scope of this accreditation.
- **NIST cybersecurity framework** provides guidance from the National Institute of Standards and Technology within the USA Department of Commerce.
  - ▶ NIST has various "special publications", such as NIST-SP-800-53, that describes security and privacy requirements for federal government and critical infrastructure.
  - ▶ A subset of GCP services is formally confirmed as compliant with these requirements.
- **COPPA** regulates the collection of personal info from children under the age of 13 in the USA.
  - ▶ COPPA rules cover, for example, parental consent for some actions.
  - ▶ "G Suite for Education" (which isn't part of GCP) contractually requires that schools using G Suite meet the COPPA parental consent requirements.
  - ▶ You may need to consider COPPA if info about children is processed by your solutions or stored in your databases.
- There are legal frameworks in various countries (e.g. GDPR or the Australian Privacy Act) that specify requirements regarding **data residency**, **data localisation** or **data sovereignty**.
  - ▶ These all relate to the location of the data centres where cloud providers store your data; whether the data needs to cross any international boundaries; and whether there's a risk that foreign governments will require the cloud provider to give them access to your data.
  - ▶ Such concerns are one of the reasons you choose by yourself in which locations your GCP services are provisioned. See table 3 (p17) for an overview of the geography of GCP services.

Chapter 10
System operation

10.1 Continuous delivery

The rise of cloud technology is linked to the trend of replacing traditional IT infrastructure with a virtualised layer, that behaves like hardware but is actually software. It still needs hardware to run on, but much more of the work is done by software engineers, leaving the direct interaction with hardware to the specialists that build the infrastructure itself. This change led to the rise of DevOps (or WebOps). DevOps is about using software to automate areas of work which were traditionally more manual. It's also about using this software-based approach to help teams collaborate easily, deliver their solutions faster, and remain cool and agile even if the requirements keep changing.

Google don't make much use of the term "DevOps", but they are still very serious about the principles of DevOps. Sometimes they do it under their own title, **site reliability engineering** (**SRE**), although SRE is sometimes more focused on the way Google run their own data centres. Some GCP services that provide DevOps capabilities are included in the Google Cloud **Operations Suite**, or "**Ops Suite**" in short. Until recently it was called **Stackdriver**.

Whichever way they're branded, services that help you efficiently develop and operate your GCP solutions are reviewed in this chapter. I'll start with services you can use during the development lifecycle, aiming to make the release process as automated as you want it to be.

Cloud Source Repositories is a private Git repository for your source code, which you can host on GCP.
- You use it for collaborative development work on the code for your GCP solutions (e.g. for GAE or GCE).
- You need an account with GitHub or Bitbucket. You can start a new repo in Cloud Source Repositories, or alternatively connect and sync to an existing one in GitHub or Bitbucket.
- You can use a "source browser" to view and search repo files.
- You can create multiple repos for a single project.

- Cloud Source Repos automatically send logs to Cloud Logging.
- It gives you the option to use "security key detection", to block your "git push" if it contains sensitive info.

Cloud Deployment Manager is the GCP service implementing the concept of **infrastructure as code**.

- You use the Deployment Manager to create **configurations**. Each config describes all the resources you want to include in one deployment, written as a YAML file.
- Configs describe lists of resources. A "resource" can be a GCP service or just part of a service, e.g. instance, bucket, database. You can also define your own types of resources. Each resource can have properties.
- A config can be made of re-usable building blocks called **templates**. A template file is written in Python or Jinja2.
- A **composite type** contains multiple templates designed to work together. For example, you can use a composite type to deploy a managed instance group, a network load balancer, and the settings they need in order to work together.
- A **manifest** is a read-only object that contains the original config you provided and the actual config that was created after importing templates and fully specifying all resources. When you update a deployment, Deployment Manager generates a new manifest file.
- The **Cloud Foundation Toolkit** provides reference templates for GCP infrastructure. Templates are available for either Deployment Manager or Terraform.

Cloud Build is a service for executing your build process on GCP infrastructure, only charging you for the build time you consume.

- You select your preferred build tool from a list that includes Docker, Gradle, maven and others.
- Cloud Build can import source code from a variety of repos or storage spaces, execute your build, and produce artifacts such as Docker containers or Java archives.

- You write a build config file (YAML or JSON) to define dependencies, tests, static analysis to run, and artifacts to create.
- You can use default build steps provided by Cloud Build, use steps contributed by the user community, or define your own.
- Each build step runs in its own Docker container. Build steps can communicate with each other and share data.
- You can start builds manually using the gcloud CLI or API, or you can use the **build triggers** feature to create an automated workflow that starts new builds in response to code changes in your code repository.
- You can view your build results using gcloud, the API, or in the "build history" page in the GCP console.
- You can test your build locally first, before submitting it to Cloud Build, using the cloud-build-local tool.
- Cloud Build can help you deliver your solutions using the **GitOps** model with GKE.
  ▶ One possible way of doing this uses two Cloud Source Repos and two Cloud Build stages.
  ▶ The first repo stores app code. After every code change, the build process puts the app together, runs tests, turns it into a container image, and put it in a container repo.
  ▶ The second repo is for Kubernetes manifest code (p56). Every time a new version of the container image is created, the second build stage applies the manifest and deploys the updated app to a GKE cluster.

Cloud Composer is a managed tool for creating workflows, i.e. automated chains of tasks that run in the order you specify.
- Cloud Composer is a managed version of the open-source **Airflow**, which was originally created at Airbnb.
- We've already seen some GCP services that run workflows, such as Cloud Dataflow (p125).
  ▶ Dataflow focuses on data pipelines, and gives more attention to the range of data transformations you can perform.
  ▶ Dataflow is serverless and auto-scaling, so it's a strong candidate to use when the amounts of data you'll need to process are highly variable.

205

- ▶ Cloud Composer has a different focus: it lets you schedule workflows which you need to run on a regular basis, so it is presented as an "orchestration" or "config as code" tool.
- You specify Cloud Composer pipelines using a Python library, and they are converted into a graph that represents your tasks and the connections between them.
- Your workflow runs on GCP but the tasks it schedules and runs can equally be based in GCP, in other clouds or on-prem.
- Behind the scenes, your workflow uses a range of GCP resources. Each Cloud Composer environment has its own resources -
  - ▶ Ops Suite is used for streaming scheduler/worker logs.
  - ▶ GKE in your own project is used to host a scheduler, worker nodes, Redis (to store worker data) and CeleryExecutor (to place your tasks in a queue).
  - ▶ GCS in your own project is used to store the workflow graph, plugins, dependencies and logs.
  - ▶ Cloud SQL in a Google-managed "tenant project" is used for IAM data and metadata.
  - ▶ GAE Flex and IAP (p186), also in the Google-managed "tenant project", are used for the Airflow web server.
- You can have more than one env per project. Each env runs in a specific zone, although it can communicate with other zones.
  - ▶ Cross-region communication with GCP services uses their public APIs.
  - ▶ VPC-native GKE clusters (p57) can be used for communicating with other resources in a VPC.
  - ▶ Cloud Composer can participate in a shared VPC (p150).

Spinnaker is a tool to make the deployment of your solutions easier whether you're using GCE, GAE or GKE.
- It's the Google version of an open-source tool which was originally created at Netflix.
- You use Spinnaker as part of your CI/CD (p11) pipeline. The Spinnaker pipeline can be triggered by Cloud Build, Jenkins, git or any other tool with automation features.
- You can include in your pipeline automated steps such as –

- ▶ Getting updated manifests from GCS and applying them to create an updated app
- ▶ Deployment to a test env and running tests
- ▶ Deployment to production if tests are successful
- ▶ Rolling out a new image to a GKE cluster when a new image has been created in the Container Registry.
- You can implement deployment patterns such as:
  - ▶ "Blue/green", i.e. having two production envs, one with the live solution and one with the previous version. Every release is made to the env not currently live, so that you can easily roll back to the previous version if needed.
  - ▶ "Canary", i.e. serving new releases to a small part of incoming traffic while comparing behaviour to the previous version. Full deployment goes ahead based on results of this analysis. Spinnaker offers automated canary analysis.
  - ▶ "Multi-cloud", i.e. deploying parts of your solution to different clouds.

Firebase Test Lab is a service that lets you test your app on devices hosted in a Google data centre.
- The Test Lab supports Android and iOS across a variety of devices and configs. The tests run on real devices.
- Test results include logs, videos and screenshots, and are available via the Firebase console.
- Test Lab runs the Espresso and UI Automator 2.0 frameworks on Android apps, and XCTest tests on iOS apps.
- Tests using these frameworks can be run through the Firebase console or the gcloud CLI.
- Android tests can be created automatically using a testing tool called **Robo**, which crawls your app and simulates the different activities users can make.

Cloud Code extends your IDE (integrated development env) to make it easier to build Kubernetes apps. It has built-in integration with Cloud Source Repositories and Cloud Build.
- Cloud Code is available for Visual Studio Code and IntelliJ.
- The focus of Cloud Code is on the code you write for your Kubernetes apps, not the code you write for config files.

- It offers ready-made Kubernetes code snippets, code auto-completion, linting (automated code checking) and debugging.
- It integrates several tools (Skaffold, Kubectl, Jib) to give the Kubernetes developer interactive feedback.
- The Skaffold tool can re-build and re-deploy your apps in real time as you make code changes.
- It also works with Kustomize, a CLI tool to combine bits of Kubernetes config from various sources into a new app. You use Kustomize to refer to existing resources and re-use them as building blocks in your new app.

Cloud Scheduler is a managed service for scheduling jobs, based on the common cron tool.
- You can use it to schedule batch jobs, repeated jobs, and retry in case of failure.
- Each job you create in Cloud Scheduler is sent to a "target" according to a specified schedule.
- The target is where the work gets executed. It can be an HTTP(S) endpoint, a Pub/Sub topic (p47), or a GAE app (p43).
- Currently, to use Cloud Scheduler, your project must contain a GAE app in one of the regions where the service is supported.

10.2 Logging and monitoring

Logging the activity in your GCP projects is critical for your ability to understand what's going on. You'll want to check your logs regularly, for example when investigating security threats or trying to understand the details of your bill. The overall logging capability across GCP services is called Cloud Logging.

Cloud Logging is part of the GCP Ops Suite (formerly Stackdriver). There are different ways to use this suite; some orgs prefer to do it separately for each project, but you can also use one account to manage your ops across different projects.

Cloud Logging is enabled by default in many services, but not all. It's not the default on GCE, where your own config determines how logging works. In GKE and GAE Flex, the containers have a native way of writing logs via the sdtout and stderr streams of the operating system, which is better to follow as a default.

Audit Logs is the heart of Cloud Logging; it includes the main log data that GCP collects for you. There are 3 types of Audit Logs: Admin Activity, Data Access, and System Event logs.

- **Admin Activity logs** record changes made to your GCP resources, such as creating VMs or changing permissions. These logs are always written; you can't configure or disable them, and there is no charge.
- **Data Access logs** record any access to your data. This includes either reading, creating or changing data, and also covers resource metadata. The logs don't include access to data that you've shared publicly. These logs are disabled by default (except for BigQuery) because they quickly get very large; so they are only written if you enable them.
- **System Event logs** record actions where Google systems (rather than users) modify the config of your resources. These logs are always written; you can't configure or disable them, and there is no charge.
- There are different ways to view your Audit Logs:
    - ▶ Via the **Logs Viewer** interface in the GCP Console, for basic project-level view.
    - ▶ On the **Activity page** of the GCP Console, for abbreviated log at project level.
    - ▶ By creating **log sink** objects, that allow you to export the logs. A sink includes a destination (which the service account has permissions to write to) and a filter query.
    - ▶ Through the Cloud Logging API
    - ▶ Through the Cloud SDK.
- To analyse your logs, you can use a basic filter (by user, resource type, date/time) or an **advanced filter** (based on conditions you put on the service, time range, metadata and other fields). The advanced filter allows you to log a random sample. The advanced filter is a feature of the Logs Viewer.
- Audit Logs record the identity that performed the logged operation. In some cases, the caller's identity is unavailable or redacted for privacy reasons.
- Default log storage is for 400 days (Admin Activity / System Event logs) or 30 days (Data Access). You pay per GB.

- Since log entries are only retained in the Ops Suite for a limited time, it's a good practice to export them and keep them in GCS or BigQuery for a longer period, either for compliance reasons or for your own analytics.
- Each project can have its own default logging, but you can create "aggregated exports" by defining log sinks that cover multiple projects, billing accounts or folders.

Access Transparency Logs are logs of the actions taken by Google staff when accessing your data.
- This includes actions you request from the support team by phone; investigations made by Google engineers following your support requests; and investigations they may initiate after an outage.
- Access Transparency logging is disabled by default. To enable it you need a suitable support package. If enabled, it applies to an entire org.

When you work with your own VMs on GCP, or other services based on GCE instances, you can choose to run a **Cloud Logging agent** on them.
- Google's recommended practice is to run such agents on all your VMs, either Linux or Windows.
- The logging agent can stream logs from third-party apps running on your VMs (Cassandra, Chef, Jenkins, MongoDB, Nginx, Tomcat and many others) to Cloud Logging.
- The logging agent is based on the Fluentd technology. It lets you configure specifically which logs get sent.
- For instances without external IPs, the log stream relies on Private Google Access (p166).
- You can also use the logging agent on AWS EC2 instances, if you set up a suitable workspace (p211) on GCP. Logs are sent to an "AWS connector project", i.e. a GCP project that connects your monitored AWS account to your workspace.
- The agent is not your first choice for any service based on containers; the native logging mechanism of the container should be your default.

- Cloud Logging records are made of **log entries**. By default, these entries are ingested as unstructured text, but when using the logging agent you can choose to create **structured logs** in JSON format.

Cloud Monitoring and Cloud Logging are best friends, but they are different things. You monitor your solutions in order to understand how they behave; you do it by collecting data, processing the data, and responding to the important parts of it. Logging is an important input into monitoring, but collecting logs isn't enough to ensure good monitoring.

Cloud Monitoring helps you continuously understand the performance, uptime, and overall health of your resources.
- You can use it for solutions you run on GCE, GAE, GKE and Pub/Sub, and also for databases and networking resources.
- You can also monitor AWS apps.
- The info you monitor is organised in **workspaces**. A workspace is a monitoring account, which can cover one or more GCP projects and/or AWS accounts. Each project can only be monitored by one workspace.
- You monitor the value of specific **metrics**. You can choose from a set of ready-made metrics or define custom metrics.
- In your workspaces you can create **uptime checks**, to verify the availability of your services by contacting them from various locations around the world.
- You can also create **alerting policies**. These policies are based on metrics you want to monitor (for example, the result of the uptime check). In the policy you define the conditions that should trigger an alert and the type of alert notification that should be sent when the conditions are met.
- You can view monitoring results in a set of pre-defined **dashboards**, or alternatively, create a custom monitoring dashboard with your chosen metrics and charts.

The **Cloud Monitoring agent** is an optional tool you can install on your VMs on either GCP (GCE) or AWS (EC2).
- The agent runs a "daemon" process on the VM, based on the **Collectd** technology, that gathers system and app metrics.

211

- The agent doesn't come with your VMs by default; you need to install it.
- By default, the agent collects disk, CPU, network and process metrics. Cloud Monitoring has partial access to these even without the agent; but the agent adds further capabilities since it can use data that is only available inside the VM, and can collect metrics from individual apps.

Error Reporting is a service that monitors errors in the code of a running service.
- You can use it with GCE, GKE, GCF, GAE, Cloud Run, and AWS EC2.
- It gives info about the error, including who's affected, how and when. It aggregates errors into meaningful groups.
- You can configure different types of notifications to be triggered by these errors.
- Supported languages include Go, Java, Node.js, PHP, Python, Ruby, dot Net.
- A similar service for Android and iOS apps is provided by **Firebase Crash Reporting**.

Cloud Trace is a service that collects latency data from GAE, HTTP(S) load balancers, and any app where you add a tracing function using the **Cloud Trace API**.
- Cloud Trace helps you understand how long it takes your app to handle incoming requests or to complete its own API calls. A *trace* is the amount of time it takes to complete a single operation.
- On GAE Standard, during runtime the env automatically sends to Cloud Trace latency info about requests to the app.
- The tracing service consists of a *tracing client*, which collects data on the app side and sends it to your GCP project, and a console interface, which lets you view and analyse this data.
- The info shown in the console interface includes performance insights, recent traces, and traces for the most frequent requests the app makes or receives.

- The console also gives you access to a "trace list" where you can examine individual traces in detail.
- Each trace consists of one or more spans. Each span is the amount of time it takes to complete a sub-operation.

Cloud Profiler is a service that performs dynamic analysis of your running apps, and shows you how their performance is influenced by specific parts of your code.
- It performs continuous profiling based on a sampling approach. Sampling provides estimated results only, but it's more suitable for live systems because data is collected periodically, with low impact on performance.
- Profiling your code while the system is live can help responding to use cases you were not aware of during development. You can of course also use profiling during development and testing, to help optimise your design.
- The data collection is done by a "profiling agent" that you add to your code. A different agent runs on each instance.
- Profiles may look into one or more of the following -
    - ▶ CPU time: the time spent running a block of code.
    - ▶ Wall time: includes the CPU time, wait time for database access lock, wait for thread sync, and other wait times. This could indicate a resource bottleneck.
    - ▶ Heap: how much heap memory is taken.
    - ▶ Allocated heap: how much memory in total is allocated, including memory no longer in use. This may indicate inefficient use of memory.
    - ▶ Threads: the number of threads an apps creates, which may indicate various blockages or inefficiencies.
    - ▶ Contention: the amount of time spent waiting for access to shared resources. This, too, can indicate that the app may be using resources inefficiently.
- Profiling results refer to specific blocks of code, to make it easier to focus on the root cause of performance issues.
- Cloud Profiler displays profiling data as Flame Graphs.
    - ▶ These graphs describe the call stack of a block of code, i.e. the collection of sub-routines executed by this block, together with profile metrics for these sub-routines.

- ▶ The flame graph is a stack of horizontal bars; the width of each bar represents a metric such as CPU time.
- ▶ When going from the top of the graph to the bottom, each level breaks down the previous level into further detail of the calls it makes or sub-routines it runs.
- ▶ When going from top to bottom, the overall width of the bars reduces, since the different calls made as part of one block of code will take less resource than the entire block.
- You can profile apps written in Go, Java, Node.js or Python. They can be deployed to GCP or anywhere else. The profiles available depend on the programming languages.

Cloud Debugger is a service that lets you inspect the state of a running app, in real time, with minimal impact on users.
- It can be used with apps already running in production, by taking a snapshot of their state.
- The snapshot captures the call stack and variables at a specific location in the code, the first time any instance executes it.
- You can also use Cloud Debugger to insert logging instructions ("logpoints") into a running app.
- You can share a debug session with others.

10.3 Resource catalogs

Another important aspect of effective ops is listing your services and resources, or specific types of resources, in an agreed place. This can help you establish a way of working where anything can be searched and found easily; nothing gets lots; the history of these resources is documented with proper version control; and much of this can be handled automatically.

We've already spoken about Cloud Source Repositories (p203), Container Registry (p60), GitHub and Docker Hub. These are all examples of this concept. Below are several other services used for listing resources.

Data Catalog is an interface for searching for data assets, currently in its Beta release.

- It can help with data discovery, management and governance.
- You can search data fields and metadata, including info about the project, dataset, schema and labels.
- You can also create a type of metadata called **tag templates**, especially for the purpose of making it searchable in the catalog across your different types of data assets.
- Data Catalog integrates with DLP (p187), so that you can use the DLP data categories in your searches.
- With the current Beta release, Data Catalog only works with built-in metadata in BigQuery (datasets, tables and views) and with Pub/Sub topics.

Private Catalog is a service you can use to make your own solutions and services available for discovery by a specified audience. It is currently in a Beta release.

- The catalog has two APIs: a **Producer API**, for admins to manage the catalog, and the general **Private Catalog API**, for users to discover solutions.
- You can use org policies (p24) and other constraints to control who can view and access different solutions in the catalog. This means you only can keep just one catalog if you prefer, even if you work with different markets or audiences.

The **GCP Marketplace** is a library of third-party packages, both free and paid, which are designed for GCP and can run on GCP with relatively simple config.

- It was previously known as Cloud Launcher and was recently re-branded.
- It offers implementations of popular stacks; popular ones include WordPress-related services and various NoSQL databases.
- If also offers bespoke apps from different vendors, which are intended to run on GCP.
- When using commercial apps from the Marketplace, billing can be handled through your GCP invoice. This can significantly reduce your admin burden.

215

Chapter 11
Exam preparation

13.1 Exam case studies

If you are preparing for Google's Professional Cloud Architect exam, you need to become familiar with 3 case studies that some exam questions will refer to. The full description of the case studies is on the GCP website, and is also available during the exam; but you should very much memorise it in advance anyway, because you will not have enough time to review it during the exam.

All 3 case studies are about orgs that consider making more comprehensive use of GCP services. I will not repeat here the full description, but here are some points which I find important about each case study.

The **Mountkirk Games** case study is about a new online game. The biggest issues are performance and scalability in real time.
- Much of the demand is from mobile users. Their requests might arrive with a delay.
- Users can be anywhere in the world, and their numbers may be unpredictable.
- Several managed NoSQL data solutions are needed:
  - ▶ To store transactions that change the state of each player
  - ▶ To handle the evolution of the game as a time series
  - ▶ To ingest streaming data, perform analytics and calculate KPIs.
  - ▶ To allow queries to access over 10 TB of historical data.
- Users may upload their own files.
- The game backend should be on GCE.

The **Dress4Win** case study is about an e-commerce platform. A key feature here is that this will remain a hybrid solution, combing cloud and on-prem, in the near future.

- It's about a web-based company with web and mobile apps, and a social network to connect users to designers and sellers.
- Their income is based on several types of activity - sales, advertising, referrals, and a "freemium" model.
- Demand has peaks at certain times of the day and the week; in the off-peak systems have low utilisation.
- Their current technology stack is complex, with hundreds of servers and appliances, all in one data centre but growing fast.
- The data centre runs one MySQL server, many servers for micro-services, static content servers, a Hadoop/Spark cluster, RabbitMQ messaging servers, Jenkins, and other DevOps and networking functions.
- Current on-prem storage includes some server-attached HDDs, iSCSI for VM hosts, SAN for the MySQL database, and NAS for images/logs/backups.
- The plan is to first migrate development, testing, disaster recovery and failover to the cloud, with private connections from the data centre to the cloud. They are not sure what changes are needed before migration.
- The main live systems should migrate later, but before the next time they need to refresh their on-prem hardware.
- The broad objectives include reliability, security, flexible provisioning of new resources, and an overall cost reduction of 35% to 50% within 5 years.

The **TerramEarth** case study is an Internet of Things (IoT) scenario, with a data source that has limited connectivity.
- It's about a company that makes vehicles for mining and agriculture. They work with 500 dealers in 100 countries.
- The agriculture business is now a small part of the business (just 20%) but it grows fast.
- They operate 20 million vehicles. The vehicles collect data and store it locally. It gets downloaded during vehicle service. The same port in the vehicle is used for both downloading and updating software.
- 200K of the vehicles (1%) are connected to a cellular network and allow more direct data collection. 120 data fields are collected per second per vehicle, 22 hours/day, adding up to 9 TB per day.

- They currently run both Linux and Windows systems in one data centre in west US.
- Data from the vehicles, in the form of zipped CSV files, is sent via FTP and uploaded to a data warehouse. It has a single Postgres server and storage with no redundancy.
- The warehouse is used for generating reports. Due to offline and/or manual steps in the data workflow, reports are based on 3-week-old data.
- The warehouse also helps plan the stock of replacement parts, with the objective of minimising vehicle downtime. They've already reduced it by 60%, but the wait for replacement can still take up to 4 weeks.
- From a team of 10 analysts (split between the east and west coasts), only 2 can use the reporting app at a time, since licenses are tied to physical CPUs.
- There are business ambitions to reduce vehicle downtime to less than a week; give dealers better insight on how customers use their equipment; predict customer needs; and build partnerships with suppliers in the agriculture market.
- Technically, the company wants to operate more data centres for low-latency coverage of the US; improve the backup strategy; secure the data transfer from the vehicle; innovate and improve skills.

13.2 Exam tips

I've included below my top tips for those preparing for the Professional Cloud Architect exam. My tips aren't about the topics that the exam covers – this has been covered throughout this book. The aspect I'm trying to cover in these suggestions is how to approach the exam questions and where the traps might be.

- **Types of questions**. Exam success requires being prepared for questions of different types –
    - ▶ The easiest questions are those that focus on a specific GCP service: each of the possible answers says something about this service, and only one of the options is true. Such questions are the easiest because all you need is

knowledge of key features of the relevant service; the info in this book is probably sufficient for this.

  ▶ The much harder questions are where you are given a problem, and each possible answer describes a different way of solving it, with a different mix of GCP services and features. The difficulty isn't about your knowledge but about time: for each of the possible answers you need to understand a different suggested solution, so you have multiple solutions to assemble in your own mind, within the time allocated to one question.

  ▶ So, when planning how you split your time, bear this in mind. Don't split time equally between questions, but plan more time for questions that require thinking about multiple solutions.

- **The obvious answer**. In many questions, some of the options seem at first glance as the obvious answer. Confusingly, sometimes they really are the right answer and it really is as simple as that, while in other cases this is a trap, and there's a more subtle detail that makes all the difference. In other words, the questions vary significantly in their level of difficulty, and nobody tells you in advance which questions are the tricky ones. Here are some examples –

  ▶ The TerramEarth case study is about an IoT business. This doesn't mean IoT Core is the right answer to whatever they ask. But they can definitely ask specific questions where IoT Core is a good solution.

  ▶ In a question that describe continuous delivery pipelines, using Deployment Manager would seem a natural fit. But if the scenario is about deploying small services that can be updated and rolled back quickly, then a pipeline that relies on GKE and Container Registry might be a better answer, even if it requires more custom config.

  ▶ In questions about logging system events you'd easily be tempted to choose answers that mention Cloud Logging or the Ops Suite. In some cases this would be right. But there are scenarios where the requirement is to process time series data, which just happens to be referred to as a log, and a database like Bigtable would be a stronger candidate.

- **Solution vs justification**. Many questions are about the right solution for a certain scenario and also about the reasons why this is the right solution. The answers to choose from can be incorrect in different ways:

- ▶ A good solution, but the reasoning isn't right.
- ▶ A correct justification, but it's attached to a bad solution.
- ▶ An answer where everything is true, but it doesn't address the requirement explained in the question.

- **The GCP geography**. Defining the right geographical scope for your solution – global, regional, zonal, or any other mix of the options in table 3 (p17) – can be simple if this is what the question is about. But the geographical context can sometimes be more subtle. For example, you may need to limit access to your data from other regions in order to meet regulatory requirements (p199). In some cases, a hidden geographical consideration will determine which answer is right.

- **Services that work together**. Some combinations of GCP services are often used as part of the same technology stack. You should be familiar with these so that you can quickly identify a good match when you see one.
    - ▶ Sometimes services make a good pair when one feeds the other as part of a common pipeline. For example, Pub/Sub with Dataflow; or Dataflow with Bigtable; or BigQuery with Data Studio.
    - ▶ Sometimes services make a good pair when they work in parallel and complement each other by addressing different cases or different types of data. For example, Dataflow with Dataproc; or BigQuery with GCS.
    - ▶ Sometimes services make a good pair when one triggers the work of the other. For example, Cloud Monitoring with GCF; or IoT Core with Pub/Sub; or GCS with GCF.
    - ▶ Some pairs don't work well together and you're expected to recognise it. For example, Load Balancing with GAE. You should be suspicious with solutions that combine a managed service with networking infrastructure. While this combination isn't unheard of, in most cases if you use a managed service then it's because you want to avoid the need to worry about networking arrangements.

- **Universal best practices**. Not everything in the exam is about GCP. In some of the questions you are expected to demonstrate that you are familiar with some well-known principles of robust solution architecture. There may even be cases where the correct answer is one that doesn't use a GCP service. Below are some examples for non-GCP practices that you are expected to know.
    - ▶ The principle of "least privilege" (p79, p151, p182).
    - ▶ Personal data protection as in GDPR or HIPAA (p201).
    - ▶ The need to test your solution in conditions as similar as possible to those it will face when it is live.
    - ▶ The use of some universal DevOps tools such as Jenkins.
    - ▶ The risk of hotspotting (p97) when you manually select how your data is partitioned.
    - ▶ The benefit in keeping labelled data and using it to continuously build ML (p129) capabilities.
- **Hybrid solutions**. Your exam will definitely cover scenarios where your solution spans an on-prem data centre and some resources on GCP; scenarios where specific GCP services are introduced to replace specific on-prem components; and possibly some scenarios where you need to use the services of multiple cloud providers. I recommend that you browse this entire book once more, focusing specifically on the questions listed below, as a way of practicing a hybrid thinking style:
    - ▶ What kind of traditional on-prem service may be replaced by each GCP service. For example, which on-prem solution would go into which GCS storage class?
    - ▶ Whether and how each GCP service could be used in a hybrid scenario. For example, what would be the role of service accounts?
    - ▶ How each GCP service would behave if it needed to communicate with an on-prem or third-party resource. For example, which GCP services allow you to specify your own hybrid networking arrangements, and which ones don't?

- **Case studies**. The three case studies summarised in the previous section have an important trait: specific GCP services naturally lend themselves to specific case studies.
  - ▶ Understanding which services suit each case study isn't something to do during the exam. You should come to the exam having already figured out which subset of GCP services are good candidates for each case study.
  - ▶ Some are good candidates simply because the case study says that's what they intend to use.
  - ▶ In other cases, the case study has requirements which specific GCP services are tailor-made for.
  - ▶ Pay particular attention to analytics vs transactional data processing, relational vs NoSQL databases, and solutions designed for global availability.
  - ▶ Pay attention also to the difference between GCP services in terms of their auto-scaling options, backup, redundancy, disaster recover, and the way they work when not connected to a network.

Lightning Source UK Ltd.
Milton Keynes UK
UKHW021230101120
373137UK00006B/61